ARC OF
CRISIS
1979

Clete Hinton

EAGLE EDITIONS
2007

EAGLE EDITIONS
AN IMPRINT OF HERITAGE BOOKS, INC.

Books, CDs, and more—Worldwide

For our listing of thousands of titles see our website
at
www.HeritageBooks.com

Published 2007 by
HERITAGE BOOKS, INC.
Publishing Division
65 East Main Street
Westminster, Maryland 21157-5026

International Standard Book Number: 978-0-7884-4133-2

Preface

There is a conflict in our world today that may bring about a destruction of monumental consequences to the people existing on this planet. The forces of good and evil will challenge one another for survival. Believers in God must unite together to counter atheists and agnostics. There has been a balance of power in past generations that has prevented mass annihilation of the human species, but that balance in power is shifting because of apathy and indifference on part of Christians and individuals who are identified with God.

The "Arc of Crisis," is a true description of this world conflict, the central theme being the countries of the Middle East, expanding to other nations, frustrated by dictatorship and autocratic rule and the communist dominated countries, there is no individual freedom. If you are accused of a crime by the secret police, you have to prove you are innocent. They can take you away to be interrogated. They may force you to admit you are responsible for certain acts against the Marxist State, even though you are innocent. The KGB, state-run intelligence, has a section 58, which covers many facets of criminal behavior, in which they can imprison you.

In the democratic governing nations, the individual freedom is exercised, and you are innocent until proven guilty. Democracy is a government run by the people, with laws and tenets that protect the common person. The populace is allowed to live in freedom and prosperity without harassment.

Section I

3-4-80

Fragile balance of power exists in international order – How
The recent attacks on our embassy are omens of a deeper division in the international order, like seismic tremors that signal the wrenching of an earthquake fault, but public apathy seems to follow even a quake of disastrous proportions.

The shift in the East-West balance has occurred gradually, as has the progress of the Soviet Unions' geopolitical influence. Some twenty years ago, the United States enjoyed large reserves of military and governmental prestige, however, the impact has shrunk on the community of nations as the capital of a rich man that delays the pain of poverty.

Referring to history in the transformation of the sphere of influence, who would have forecasted a Caribbean nation sending Soviet-equipped expeditionary forces to fight against American interests in the Middle East and Africa? In the 1950's the United States maintained a base in Libya and military facilities in Ethiopia, where now the Soviet surrogates are firmly entrenched. Our British naval base 20 years ago while today the Russian fleet is harbored in Cam Ranh Bay supplying Vietnam.

Because of this erosion in geographic assets and military strength, the West's capability to cope with a crisis is becoming progressively weaker, each future setback more dangerous, tilting the balance of power.

Napoleon Bonaparte completed the expansion of his vast empire from Spain to Russia within some 17 years – in an era when communications and travel were immeasurably slower than the present. Hitler's achievement on power, the collapse of the collective security system of the League of Nations, rearmament of Germany, annexing of territories and the World War which he unleashed – all of these events took place within a span of 13 years.

3-9-80
Soviet troops of ground assault capability appear in Indian Ocean

The Soviet Union may be sending ground assault forces to the Indian Ocean aboard ships, according to reliable intelligence sources.

Amphibious combat units of the Russian nation were aboard a 13,000-ton Rogov, the largest Soviet amphibious vessel, reported to be carrying armored personnel carriers and air cushioned landing craft.

The Russian navy now has over thirty attack ships in the Indian Ocean-Arabian Sea area. Many of the naval fleet of the United States and the Red nation are within striking distance of the entrance to the Persian Gulf, one of the chief sources of oil supplies for the Western country, including Europe and Japan.

There have been no hostile actions on either side. However, political tensions have risen since the Soviet occupation of Afghanistan in late December and President Carter warned that the United States would resist any Russian attempt to gain control of the entrance to the Red Sea and the oil rich states of the Middle East.

3

3-20-80
North Yemen mystifies the super powers
Sana, North Yemen

As the King of Siam use to say, it is a puzzlement. No one seems to know what is going on in Yemen, but it is strategically important to both the Western contingent and the Red Communities.

North Yemen is an extraordinary country, a legendary land of seven to eight million wild tribesmen whose people are craggy and lean and tough as mountains they live in. Its borders ring Saudi Arabia, and its seashores could blockade the Red Sea.

When the Russians, with East Germans, and Cubans assumed control of South Yemen in 1970, they migrated to the north. The wily Yemenis accepted the gifts from the Communists of armored tanks and military equipment to improve their fighting strength. When the United States offered to give 390 million dollars worth of arms to fight the Communist South, the Prime Minister Abdul Azis Abdul-Ghani was grateful, and said, "Sure, we will stand with the Americans."

Northern officials stress that a government of a president elected by two legislative councils elected by the people, based in Sana, would rule the two-countries-in-one. The constitution would be based on Islam.

A three-month dispute with neighboring Saudi Arabia has been resolved with North Yemen sending its 100 Soviet advisors home. Egyptian sources said, "Yemen has agreed not to merge with South Yemen, a Marxist State." It will send 120 of its citizens scheduled to study in Moscow to Pakistan instead. In return, Saudi Arabia will resume financial aid to North Yemen, beginning with 300 million dollars to pay for American Arms.

4-1-80
The United States must alter the leadership of the Soviet Union

Hoping to deter future Soviet aggression, the American government is threatening a major military response, increasing defense spending, renewing a draft registration, rapid deployment of armed forces, and talking to the Chinese government of military commitments concerning the Red Russians. We need to restructure the issues to make it appear that the Soviet Union agrees to our actions or inaction.

We should redefine the parties to the dispute in Afghanistan. The Soviets invasion must be seen as against the non-aligned Islamic World. The funding for the Afghan freedom fighters can be from Saudi Arabia or Kuwait, not the United States.

We should condemn the conduct of the Communist nation, not the country. In political costs, we should maximize the pain and suffering from restrictions of technology transfers, wheat sales, diplomatic contacts and the Olympics. The suffering of international prestige will do more to destroy the Russians than any other single penalty, and in the eyes of bi-lateral countries and non-aligned nations will deteriorate confidence and trust of the surrogates and satellites.

4

Red Communists of Russia fear Islamic unification
Moscow

The current struggle in Afghanistan is not the first the Kremlin has waged against Muslim rebels bent on preserving their way of life. There was a similar clash in the years following the 1917 Revolution that brought the Communists to power, when the Bolsheviks under Lenin were moving to consolidate Soviet rule over the Central Asian peoples who had been subjugated by the Czars of Russian.

Some experienced diplomats concede that the Kremlin are using the same tactics today in Afghanistan, and throughout the Islamic world.

The Basmachi Rebellion, (The Oppressed), erupted in the region of the Caspian Sea east to the frontier of China and Mongolia. The rebels, like their Afghan counterparts of today were disorganized and ill-equipped, but their guerrilla tactics were effective. They kept the Red Army on the run for more than a decade.

The Basmachis were made up of partisan detachments almost exclusively on horseback. They were elusive and often dissolved into the neighboring villages literally before the eyes of the Soviet troops.

Today, hundreds of thousands of Afghan refugees have made their way across international borders to tribal lands in Pakistan and Iran. Some of them seek only a respite before returning to fight the Communists in their homeland.

In the end, the Basmachi Rebellion was crushed. The men in the Kremlin did it with brutal force, combined with periodic concessions to national customs that masked, but did not alter their goal, of destroying the Islamic foundation.

The Basmachi movement never attained its ultimate purpose, to overthrow the Russian rule in Turkestan, because the Communists were infinitely better organized, and had at their disposal a larger and more experienced armed force. What is needed today is the unification of the Islamic people to attack the aggressor nation.

Cuban Communists infiltrate Granade
As Havana reaps the benefits of the American neglect of the Caribbean region, a growing Cuban presence permeates that vital area. Strong Castro influence in Jamaica, the Cuban-sponsored Sandinista victory in Nicaragua and the Communist coup in Gradada underline the passivity of the United States. Diplomats of the small speaking English nations scattered throughout the Caribbean now fear their countries may be the scourge of the Cuban dictator.

Slightly more than a year ago, a Castro-sponsored coup toppled the government of Granada, a small island paradise, independent since 1974. Although known primarily as a producer of nutmeg spice and a haven for American, German, and Canadian sun seekers, Granada straddles the vital shipping lanes through which oil tankers and merchant ships pass. Populated by over 100,000 people, the island lies astride the oil fields of Venezuela and Trinidad, and near the refinery facilitates in the Netherland Antilles.

Using Cuban commandos as a battering ram, the New Jewel Movement, a socialist assemblage led by Maurice Bishop, seized power in March 1979, brought down the government of Dir Eric Gairy, and replaced it with a police state. Today the (New Jewel Movement) governs the Peoples Revolutionary of Granada. In order to assume total control over the people, Premier Bishop has established committees for the defense of the Revolution – local block committees coordinated by the secret police. Members of Havana's intelligence supervise these groups.

While having predictably friendly relations with Cuba and the East Bloc, the Grenada regime has frightened the smaller independent nations surrounding it. Barbados, a prosperous pro-West island state, could find itself recipient of subversion. Unless the United States and residual British influence in the Caribbean awaken and realistically tackle the situation, they may be absorbed.

Frontier of the Strait of Hormuz is the state of Oman
Strait of Hormuz

The Omani information officer, Abdul Aziz Rawwas states, "With Russians in the Horn of Africa, in South Yemen, and in Afghanistan, we are seeing the expansion of a new colonial power."

The Soviet Union has taken control of the military headquarters in Aden Arabia, and Red officers command South Yemen army units down to battalion level, East Germans run internal security apparatus, and 4,000 Cubans are involved in everything from training the militia to flying Soviet-made Mig-21 fighters.

Under the terms of a 20-year friendship agreement signed last October between Moscow and Aden, the Kremlin has brought surveillance jets to the region, developed dry dock facilities to service up to 12 submarines at one time, and house and support several thousand men.

The Oman regime would like the Western democratic nation to provide military capability, particularly anti-aircraft and anti-tank weapons, and assurances of U.S. action in the event of a Soviet threat to the Straits of Hormuz.

The Sultan of Oman, Kaboos ibn-Saud, speaks out, "We feel that the United States can and should stop the Russians from achieving their goals in the gulf."

Oman shield against Soviet Union for the West
Muscat, Oman

The United States and Oman have completed the first phase of negotiations toward a new military alliance that will allow the North American nation to use bases near the Persian Gulf in exchange for a commitment to defend Oman.

The two countries have reached basic agreement on a new phase that will give the U.S. Air Force access to three Omani air bases, one of them within 240 miles of the Strait of Hormuz. The United States navy will be granted facilities at Oman's two ports.

In return the American nation will pay for improvements to the air and naval bases, supplying the armed forces of Oman with new weaponry and a pledge to defend the Arab principality in event of alien attack.

The U.S. Navy task forces patrolling the waters south of Iran are at present using Oman for re-supply. Small aircraft from the aircraft carriers Nimitz and Coral Sea fly in and out of Muscat ferrying mail and perishables. The Carter

Administration would like to develop a U.S. Rapid Deployment force in the region of over 20,000 men.

The government of Oman has asked Washington for anti-tank missiles, C-130 transport planes, anti-aircraft radar and missile systems, gunboat and minesweepers to help patrol the 24 mile-wide strait for defense purposes.

Israel offers military bases to the United States
Prime Minister Menachem Begin of Israel states that the American government should have conventional military forces in the Middle East and "If you want facilities in our country, we shall put them at your disposal."

Begin declared that in the light of the hostage crisis in Iran and Soviet intervention in Afghanistan, "The United States must have conventional forces on the spot, not to bring them from afar in emergency situations. The Western power is our friend and ally, and we will do all that is possible to preserve peace and the balance of power. The Communists are infiltrating throughout this explosive theatre of operations. The Russians, now in Afghanistan can travel through Baluchistan and can reach the Indian Ocean with no major military presence to stop them. Iran, itself, may become a Communist State with the Tudeh Party, an organized group . . . waiting. The Tudeh Party supports Khomeini because he has humiliated the United States, and the costs are great, in honor and judgement in the world at large.

Saddam Hussein, Strongman of Iraq
Baghdad, Iraq
Critics, mindful of the foes executed by the score, call him the "Butcher of Baghdad." Supporters say, that more than any other Arab leader, he eschews visionary goals. He is stereotyped "The Engineer of Revolution."

Many considerations favor Saddam as the fulcrum of the Middle East melting pot of confusion. A reputation as a revolutionary has given Hussein an opening to the "progressive regimes in Syria, Libya, South Yemen, and Algeria. A strong army, and commandos for hire, put him in a position to threaten and protect Saudi Arabia, Kuwait, and the weaker sheikdoms of the Persian Gulf.

Success initially crowned the Iraqi bid for leadership. At summit meetings in Baghdad in 1978 and last year, most of the nations of the Arab terrorist states joined Iraq in condemning Egyptian President Anwar Sadat's 'separate peace" with Israel. On March 8, 1980, Saddam issued an eight-point Arab charter, designed to hold Russia and the United States out of the Persian Gulf, while casting Iraq in a leading role as the protecting power of the region.

In Tripoli, in the early part of April, at a conference the Syrian President met with other radical heads of state from Libya, Algeria, South Yemen, and the Palestine Liberation Organization to affirm the strongest possible stance against the Egyptian-Isreali peace accords.

This action by Arab revolutionaries results in a three-way split in the Moslem world; Sadat, moving toward settlement with Israel under American auspices; Hussein, pushing for the non-aligned grouping of Arab nations; and the radical current, led by Syria with support from the Kremlin from Russia.

Superpowers keenly aware of nuclear arms annihilation
Military force is clearly a major reality, but three factors inhibit its use by the United States and the Soviet Union in the present post-Afghanistan era: the

world-wide availability of modern weapons, volatile nationalism, and the irrelevance of combat in many international situations.

There are five acknowledged nuclear-weapons states. India has exploded a nuclear device, Israel and South Africa are troubling question marks. Potential new members of the nuclear club are to be found mainly in the Third World. Guerillas, saboteurs, and terrorists can paralyze and impede invading armies.

Nationalism represents a powerful deterrent, as Washington discovered in Vietnam, and Moscow is learning in Afghanistan. A country with ideals and fierce determination will resist foreign domination. Also subversion by the Russians of a free independent nation has alienated the non-aligned countries, enraged the Moslems, and antagonized the Western superpower.

In many events the use of armed force is irrelevant. The United States could not use it to free the hostages in Iran. The Red Communists did not prevent China from invading Vietnam, nor block the peace treaty between Japan and China, or prevent Pope Paul from reaching the Polish faithful in which millions of people renounced the atheists of the Kremlin, yielding to a higher power of God.

If peace in the world is to continue, a balance of power must be maintained. A way to keep this balance is to plan, develop, and work for harmony by exchanging technology and automation, space and medical breakthroughs, in the years to come.

Arabs pressure Oman to bring about Moslem unity
The Sultanate of Oman, the United States ally on the Persian Gulf, has been the odd man out of the Arab world. It is the only country on the Arabian Peninsula ready to accept American personnel, the only one who has supported Egypt in its effort to make peace with Israel, the only one with virtually no direct relations with the Palestine Liberation Organization.

The United States is negotiating a military pact with Kaboos ibn-Saud at the precise moment when his nation is moving closer to its Arab cousins – and that may create tensions for both the Sultan and his friends of the West.

The Omanis practice a separate kind of Islam. They remain adherents of the Ibadhi sect, described as "Quakers of Islam, bereft of a clergy."

The United Arab Emirates have financed roads across the Omani desert, with a clear means of travel from Muscat to Abu Dhabi, television satellite communication, and technology to reach the modern countries of our globe.

Demands from the Palestinians may cause the Sultan to quietly withdraw his support of the Camp David accord. As a first step toward a comprehensive settlement, including the Palestinian autonomy, Oman concurred it was a good plan, but should it fail, the people of Oman would pressure the Sultan to rejoin the rest of the Arab rejectionists.

The monarchies are unlikely to be bedfellows for Baghdad's radical socialists, but the forces of evil never give up. The nations of the Mideast must be constantly on the alert against any foreign intervention.

Senitinals of the Strait of Hormuz
Baluchistan

One of the least known wars in modern history ended in November 1977, in the hills and valleys of Southwestern Pakistan.

The war pitted the Pakistan army against an indomitable tribal people, the Baluchis, whose homeland stretches from the Indus River west across Pakistan into southeastern Iran and the plateau of southern Afghanistan. The Baluchis are the guardians of the Persian Gulf, sentinels of the Strait of Hormuz. Of the more than four million Baluchis, the frontiers ostensibly separate them and render them citizens of neighboring nations, the people come and go at will, beholden only to their fierce and warlike traditions. The men wear tunics and baggy trousers of rough homespun cloth. A turban is worn on their head, one long end of cloth trailing across the face and onto the shoulder. They are shod in homemade slippers; their toes turned up. Many men carry rifles, fashioned by tribal armorers, working at forges deep in the rugged hills. The women, if they are to be seen at all, are swathed in the robes of the purdah (veil or curtain), their faces often covered with elaborate lacework masks to hide them from the eyes of men.

These clanish people often are seen driving camel trains through border passes. The Baluchi camel was especially bred centuries ago for lightening like raids on northern trade routes, when banditry was common in the region.

Historically, the people are nomadic, although their ways do not permit roaming too far from their small holdings. They reside on cooperative farms, raising wheat, barley, fruit and vegetables, which by custom must be maintained the year round, or else the owners lose claim to the produce. There is a certain permanence to a Blanch camp, the tents of black goat hair, or palm fronds.

The wise old Saddars, (Tribal leaders), detest the Russian Communism striving for national identity and a national homeland.

No solution for the Red Bear after five months in Afghanistan
New Delhi

Five months after the Soviet invasion of Afghanistan, no real progress has been made toward settling the crisis, despite the fact that everyone involved wants it consummated.

Because of its own Islamic fervor, Iran more than Pakistan has championed the cause of Muslim guerillas in Afghanistan, but a change of attitude has taken place in the past few weeks to resolve the differences between the Russians and the Islamic nations. The low profile military presence that has characterized Soviet occupations of Hungary and Czechoslovakia has been impossible in Afghanistan, Anti-Soviet feeling continues to mount as insurgency escalates. The public contempt for the President, Karmal and his Marxist regime has spread throughout the country.

The Politburo would like a treaty which would put an end to the use of Pakistani and Iranian border areas as rebel sanctuaries, prior to any troop withdrawal. But the beleaguered Karmal regime has virtually no popular support and would be seized by the Moslem zealots as soon as the Russians vacated. International guarantees for a government that does not have the strength to survive internal opposition is meaningless.

Historically, the Soviet Union has been willing to live with a stable, friendly, but non-Communist government in Afghanistan, which was ruled by a monarchy until it was brought down in 1973. The last king, Zahir Shah, is reported by some circles in Afghanistan, to be favored in bringing order to a volatile nation, and who could be followed by the masses. Shah, who is in his middle 60", lives in Rome, Italy.

Unless the Kremlin unleashes a massive military operation to support Karmal, they will have no alternative but to negotiate a real truce with Moslem leaders, establishing a provisional regime that would convene a Loya Jirga, ground council of Elders (Tribal).

Kremlin methodically increases presence in Afghanistan

Despite new evidence showing popular support to resist Soviet invasion of Afghanistan, the widening split in the Western alliance is making it difficult for the American administration to exploit what ought to be an opportunity to pressure the Russians to withdraw from the invaded country.

There is rapid disintegration and reliability from the invaded country. Afghan army, assassination of pro-Soviet officials, and growing enforcement of the rebel nationalists, but Western Europe – especially the Red Bear marches with unrelenting fury into the central plains of the Moslem country.

Administration officials say that even foreign embassies of Afghanistan are "completely subservient" and responsive to Soviet ambassadors in each capital of the world. The Kremlin does not contemplate any reduction of force, in fact they are brainwashing Afghan youths with new style textbooks, molding education to fit Moscow's view of history in the hopes of building a pro-Soviet generation for the future.

There have been reports that a major reinforcement of 85,000 Russian troops fighting in Afghanistan is about to occur. With the West split in its response of military aggression outside the Warsaw Pact since World War II, the Kremlin is proceeding slowly, but methodically. This condition would not have been possible with a united Western Alliance.

Limited Soviet withdrawal from Afghanistan not acceptable
New Delhi, India

The Russians announced a limited withdrawal of combat troops from the Moslem country supported by a pro-Communist regime. The condition that remains with the Marxist is so chaotic that it is virtually impossible for the Russians to leave without losing face.

Some pressure might be applied to curtail the modest flow of supplies to Pakistan based insurgent groups, but the impact would be marginal. The Muslim nation is conservative and largely uncoordinated. Many of the weapons for the insurgents are captured from, or handed over to them by demoralized and defeated Afghan army units.

Unlike the American presence in the Persian Gulf, the Soviets cannot simply decide that they had made a mistake, and withdraw totally. The two countries share a 1200-mile common border. The Russians perceive instability and a hostile government as a direct threat to the security of their own heavily Moslem southern republics.

Until the Kremlin can find someone acceptable to both themselves and to the Afghan people, Soviet military occupation will remain in Afghanistan.

Retrenching from a major military commitment is far more difficult than entering it in the first place.

Russians shuttle launch demonstrates progress of Salut

The Soviet Union launched the Soyus 37 on July 23, 1980, and returned to earth on August 1, 1980 with a Vietnamese cosmonaut on board as a guest attraction.

The selection of Lieutenant Colonel Pham Tuan, came as a surprise, since the Vietnamese joined the cosmonaut program only last summer. His 12-month training and preparation was barely sufficient to teach him the rudiments of spacecraft control, emergency procedures and space station living practices.

The nationality of each guest cosmonaut is presumed to have diplomatic significance. Tuan, who is credited with shooting down an American B-52 bomber in 1972, is a symbol of Russian influence on Vietnamese military affairs, and spent half his adult life of 33 years in Russian military schools.

The first group of foreign cosmonauts reported to Moscow in December 1976, and made space flights in 1978. In March of that year, Vladmir Remek of Czechoslovakia visited Salut 6. Next was Miroslaw Hermaszewski from Poland who followed in June. That August, Sigmund Jaehn of East Germany followed. A second group of cosmonauts reported for training in March 1978, the first of them, Georgi Ivanov of Bulgaria, made a space flight in April 1979, followed by Bertalan Farkas of Hungary a year later.

Other pilots in the Soviet space program will include France, North Korea, Ethiopia, Afghanistan, South Yemen, Sweden, Finland, and possibility the Palestinian Liberation Organization contingent.

The mechanical endurance of the Salut has been impressive as the human endurance aboard the space laboratory. Most of the photographic surveys and materials, processed in onboard furnaces, have gone to organizations for industrial application, not for research. Onboard life support systems have involved sophisticated equipment for recycling water and for growing food crops. Soviets desire to establish permanently manned space stations.

Communist Poland at historic crossroad

There are hard-liners in the Polish Marxist Party who are as rigidly orthodox as the Russian leadership, and who can be expected to flaunt a Soviet threat in an attempt to block reforms that may decrease the Kremlin prestige. The Communist leader of Poland, Edward Gierek has eliminated some of the most powerful Reds of the Politburo, and he does seek a compromise for freedom among the labor organizations to establish their own unions, separate from the Kremlin Party domination.

Hungary in 1956 and Czechoslovakia in 1968 indicated the outer limits of Russian tolerance for diversity and experiment in the Soviet bloc. The Red Army moved when Budapest tried to leave the Warsaw Pact and proclaim neutrality. It moved again when Prague tried to share the power of a single ruling party. The real reason for Soviet intervention in Prague was Moscow's fear that the Communists were losing their monopoly of control and privilege.

The only way the Polish workers movement can be put down is by direct force of the Russian mechanized forces, and that would be the definitive, historical, end of Communism as an ideology in Europe and in industrial nations.

11

If liberalism is achieved and the Poles improve their system, Hungary, Czechoslovakia, East Germany will follow and the Soviet system of Marxism will become fractious. Either way, Poland now is at an historic crossroad. The direction it takes will have a broad and long impact on much of the world.

Different ideologies create confrontation between Iran and Iraq – How Conflict between Iraq and Iran was unavoidable following the overthrow of the Shah, with the introduction of the Ayatollah Khomeini, who challenges the very survival of the ruling Baath government in Baghdad.

Mass participation in the Baath's activities has been generally lacking and the party's ideals have remained oblivious to the lives most ordinary Iraqis. Both party manifesto and party structure are regarded as screens disguising the naked power of a small group of men – most of who are from a region, Tikrit, north of Baghdad.

Alienation of two-thirds of the population on ethnic and religious grounds gives the regime an almost paranoic sense of insecurity. The depth of the Baathists insecurity was revealed recently when President Saddam Hussein embarked on a campaign of propaganda and public relations to achieve an image as "Man of the people."

At the same time, Hussein had every reason to believe that the Iranian authorities were seeking through subversion among Iraq's Shia Muslims his overthrow. The attempted assassination of Tarik Azziz, an Iraqi vice premier and member of the evolutionary Command Council, in April 1980, by the Iranian-sponsored Da'wa guerillas frightened the Baathists, and aggravated Hussein's apprehension for the safety of his regime. He began to adopt attack as the best form of defense. Early this month, in September, 1980, Hussein's forces seized 80 square miles of Iranian territory, and set a presence for escalation into full scale war.

Last April the Baath put to death Bakr Sadr, Ayatollah Khomeini's close follower in the Iraqi Shia community. The Iranian leader neither forgot nor forgave the Iraqi government for this subversive act, or for the neglect of him, Khomeini, during his long exile in Iraq and for his summary expulsion in 1978 at the behest of the Shah.

Iraq's invasion of Iran coldly deliberate
Before Saddam Hussein had officially taken over the presidency of Iraq, a high-ranking member of his government had been overheard complaining about the regime. He was seized by the secret society, along with sixty-seven other men, including some of the nation's best and most intelligent; arrested and charged with treason. Hussein ordered twenty-one of these men executed by a firing squad. This was in August of 1979.

For a decade, the president of Iraq has been the strongman of a country where leaders are notably short-lived and the enemy is all around. Together with the members of the Revolutionary Command Council, Hussein has accomplished a reversal of the economic and social life of the Iraqi, and dramatically, with the invasion of Iran, asserting a new leadership role for his oil-rich nation in the Persian Gulf; and throughout the Arab world.

The attack of the Iranians was no sudden decision. Saddam Hussein had been planning diplomatic support from other Moslem countries month before attacking his neighbor on September 9, 1980. The struggle between the two nations has historic and religious overtones. Some 5,000 years ago, when the land between the Tigris and Euphrates Rivers, known as Mesopotamia and its neighbor to the East was Persia, the armies of the ambitious despots crossed these borders. Murderous atrocities were created between the Shiite Muslim and the Sunni Moslem sects, reaching across the centuries to the present war.

The President of Iraq distrusts the United States, but he also respects its power and wants to be respected in turn. There is a psychological need to compete with the American country, to overwhelm them with power and trade deals. The Palestinian issue is the touchstone of Iraqi goals, and Saddam fears that Israeli expansionism will bring division in the Arab world.

Islam is a dynamic force in Indonesia
There is a striking resemblance between the countries of Iran and Indonesia; both are Muslim and both are oil producing nations. Indonesia is – as Iran was – ruled by an autocratic, military-backed government that is corrupt and repressive, and is committed to modernization.

Indonesia is experiencing an Islamic revival in search for spiritual comfort at a time when traditional values are breaking down under the impact of a capitalist framework. Statistically, Indonesia is the largest Muslim nation on earth, with ninety percent of an estimated 145 million people Islamic. The Indonesian Muslims are of the Sunni sect and are more concerned with education than political power.

President Suharto and the ruling body of the secular society is gradually being eroded by the Islamic Federation, that is becoming a vital element of the Islamic faith. Today, the Muslims see themselves as the underprivileged class, and they are frustrated and angry. There is no Arabian Muslim in the central government, and the role of educator of the Islamic leaders is minimal. Christians account for five percent of the population. They hold several key positions in the cabinet, and own two of the leading newspapers.

The expanding Islamic insurgence, political outlets steadily eroding, is causing an upheaval, and this kind of fuel could result in an explosion, of internal magnitude, that could destroy the secular government.

The United States of America must re-assert itself in the mind and heart of its universal neighbors, forgetting the past mistakes, and striving for freedom and equity, supporting all its allies, in future negotiations.

In Nicaragua, the American nation had supported the Somoza family from 1937 until the day, in 1979, when it became evident that the Anastasio Somoza regime could no longer keep order in the country. An American contingent attempted to lash together non-radical forces – at a time when political initiative had already passed to the Sandinista guerillas.

In El Salvador today, it is possible the same thing is happening. The United States has resumed military aid to the military government, but the army has experienced unit defections to the leftist insurgents. This government was originally supposed to be moderately "repressive." The North American nation does not possess the power to confer legitimacy or success upon an incompetent or failing ruler. Conversely, Democratic enmity, hostile propaganda, subversion – even invasion, in the style of "The Bay of Pigs" – will not bring down a ruler who controls his government. He does not have to be popular, simply feared.

An intelligent national policy attempts, unsentimentally, to recognize and ride the force of events. It does not speculate upon how much repression a country must endure, but stand determined to uphold freedom in all its aspect, and justice.

January 20, 1981
Ronald Reagan elected President of the United States

The National Policy of the American people and a Democratic nation have elected a new president in hopes of reducing the size of government at home, and to re-establish the continent's integrity in the eyes of the world. As the American hostages from Iran return home from their captures, the Reagan forces pledge to turn America around, and start a new beginning.

The Administration's candidates for major surgery are the Social Security benefits paid to the college-student children of deceased workers, the national system of extended unemployment benefits and the lavish subsidies paid to business and agriculture. The conventional wisdom of the experts, and the complexity of the federal government implies that not much can be done to radically change, "special interests" that have paralyzed a structured society.

For example, federal pensions, which currently consume nearly half of the nation's personnel budget. These pensions are adjusted twice each year to reflect the cost of living, which means that every three point rise in inflation rate adds to the federal deficit a half billion dollars. The solution to this problem is to kill or reduce the cost of living to a bare minimum. This premise would enrage the Retired Federal Employees and the Social Security claimants. Our Founding Fathers did more than just require a president go to Congress for approval of, or excising of the laws; they set up a legislature composed of many single-member districts so that every interest and region would have its champion. They divided the Congress into two houses with staggered Senate terms, to protect against "tyranny of the majority," by making bold government changes.

Commissions are made up of regulatory agencies, although appointments by the President are independent. They cannot be fired without due cause, or dictated to, and may be sued for interference.

The bold promises of a president, cutting the size of a bureaucracy, require slow and procedural advances.

2-8-81
Newly elected Secretary of State of the U.s. to test diplomacy between Algeria and Morocco

Alexander Haig, with a martial air, who has the brains and guile to be a superb Secretary of State, will get an early test of his diplomatic skills when he attempts to set American policy in North Africa.

The Secretary must analyze how to cultivate a new friend, Algeria, without alienating an old friend, Morocco. The two neighbors – conservative, monarchial Morocco and left-leaning socialist Algeria – have been at odds politically.

Their hostility involves a vast stretch of valuable desert called the Western Sahara. Morocco's claim to this tract of land has been contested for five years by the Polisario national liberation movement. These leftist guerillas get their strongest support from Algeria.

Before the Iranian crisis, Morocco's King Hassan was a staunch ally of the United States, who risked enmity of Arab leaders in supporting the treaty of Egypt and Israel called the "Camp David Accords."

Algeria channeled arms from the Soviet Union to the Polisario guerillas, provoking Hassan to divert military aid into the Western Sahara despite legal strictures that required Morocco to use arms for defense only.

The American nation is suddenly in the middle, due to the diplomatic service in negotiations that led to the release of fifty-two American hostages in Iran by the Algerian nation.

The analysis is: The bulk of the Polisario partisans are from the Reguibat tribe, one of the most powerful of the Saharan peoples, and the guerillas generally have the backing of the Saharan population.

The war of attrition against Morocco would evaporate without direct Algerian financing. As of today, King Hussan can contain, but not eliminate Polisario harassment.

Bending of the code between the super powers -
This is a violation of Détente agreed to in 1972, and something more fundamental – unwritten norms of mutual restraint. Military force can be used to resist change in political balance, but the unwritten law has not been to expand predominance by intervening into the government's autonomy.

The President of the Soviet Union, Leonid Brezhnev, in his opening speech of the 26th Communist Party in February 1981, indicated that he would embrace an active dialogue with the United States and President Reagan "at all levels" hoping to solve differences that has magnified to warlike confrontation.

The bending of the code of ethics between the Super Powers – What Rules for Soviet-American conflict have been unraveled. The United States and the Soviet Union agreed in 1972 to a code of conduct. In statements issued during the second week of February 1981, each accused the other of breaking the code.

The Department of State recited Russian sponsorship for the Cubans in Angola, the Ethiopian war and Afghanistan as cases of Soviet violation. The Soviet Union said that the United States has annexed the Persian Gulf and other areas to its "sphere of influence," as stage provocative military exercises.

In retrospect, the secret police of the Communist state, have privately argued that Henry Kissinger, the past Secretary of State of the American government, attempted to cut the Soviet Union out of the Middle East in the Arab-Israeli settlement of shuttle diplomacy that followed the Yom Kipper War of 1973. The Russians wanted a general conference in Geneva in which the Arab powers, Israel and the United States together with the Kremlin would decide together how to end the crisis.

Through the efforts of the President of Egypt, Anwar Sadat, and the peace-making negotiating teams of President Carter of the United States and Prime Minister Menachem Begin, the Camp David agreements were consummated without the input of the Soviet Union.

What the Middle East needed, then as now, was less superpower involvement. The rival sides have introduced factors irrelevant to the basic issues dividing Arabs from Israel. The Kremlin not only has played an unconstructive role in the Fertile Crescent, but has sponsored the Cubans in Africa, looked for political bases in Yemen and the Horn of Africa, conducted a "coup D'etat in Afghanistan, and in 1980 invaded the country.

3-8-81
Russian surrogate entrenchment endangers Latin America
Over the last 12 years, détente and rising Latin American independence have formed the background for the Soviet's emergence as an economic, political, and military force in the region. Deep rooted anti-Yankee sentiment and Cuban complicity have provided an atmosphere in which the Kremlin has pursued objectives, using sympathetic parties and guerilla organizations – and even military juntas and right-wing dictatorships.

Soviet trade with Latin America – excluding Cuba – grew ten fold between 1970 and 1977. Fully one-third of the Soviet-bloc Council for Mutual Economic Assistance (Comecon) Third World imports came from Latin America even before the Latest massive Russian wheat purchase from Argentina.

By the late 1970's the Kremlin was helping build 20 large scale Hydroelectric and thermoelectric power plans in the Spanish American nations. They are seeking an agreement with Venezuela and Mexico – thus far unsuccessfully – for triangulation of oil trade. The Soviets would supply Venezuela and Mexican customers in Western Europe, while Mexico and Venezuela would reciprocate by supplying Cuba.

Russian Hegemony is infiltrating through Mexican and Argentina connections, with technology in nuclear and radiation, offering to supply these countries with enriched uranium, metallurgy with highly advanced metallic titanium. Argentina has become the chief exporter of grain and meat to the Soviets, fostered with influential financial industrialists, administrators of army equipment and advisors. Local sympathizers who embrace Communism in a joint struggle against Western imperialism support an intelligence network.

March, 1981
Freedom fighter Saad Haddad awaits liberation of Lebanon
Major Saad Haddad, commander of about 2000 Christian and Shia militiamen, is a flag bearer and patriot of the Free Lebanese. He is a mile mannered man – courteous and reflective – intensively dedicated to his people.

Lebanon's population is about three million, evenly divided between Maronite Christians, whose spiritual leader is the Pope of Rome; and Shia Mulims (the smaller of Islam's, in most Arabian nations.) Before 1975, Lebanon was a model of Democracy, with cooperation between Christian and Muslim. Its capital, Beirut, was the financial capital of the Middle civil war, influenced by Western values, the Palestinian Liberation army terrorists pursuing its own goals, caused a complete collapse of the Lebanese army, when Syrian troops overran the territory with armored divisions supported by the Arab League. In desperation many of the people in Southern Lebanon turned to Israel for help.

Israel responded with military supplies, food, and medicine. In 1979 Haddad declared a six-mile wide belt along the Southern border under his control to be "Free Lebanon," independent of the government of Beirut. The Major battles almost every day with the PLO and Syrian insurgents.

Free Lebanon, with about 60,000 Shia and 40,000 Christians has no administration, collects no taxes, and depends on volunteers for survival. Its water comes from Israel, its electricity free from power stations in Sidon and Tyre. Gas and gasoline is supplied tax-free for 95 cents a gallon by the Israelis.

The home of Major Haddad is in Merj Uyun, with the appearance of a villa from a distance. Up close windows are broken, the outside needs repair, walls are shell ridden, sandbags are in front of doorways, and corrugated strips of metal are where roofs use to be.

Freedom fighter, Saad Haddad, awaits liberation of Lebanon

Haddad does not think of Free Lebanon as an independent country, or separated from the nation as a whole, but he and his people consider Beirut, the capital; under occupation of the entire Lebanese nation.

The Palestinians are the "Invaders to the freedom fighters, Syria is the "intruders," and the Beirut government is a "Sell Out."

The United States is the strongest country in the world, and head of the Free World, and should act like it. Allies should be able to trust the American country, to rely on their words, and enemies should respect and fear reprisals when they go too far, explained the Lebanese leader.

The ambition of the tired warrior is to see Lebanon free again. He will return to his house to live with his family of a wife and five daughters, and take care of his garden, planting flowers, and peace will be in his house.

Afghan Moujahedeen

The Moujahedeen usually strike at night, moving into the cities in groups of 40 to 50, raiding military installations or political targets, such as homes or offices of leading party officials. Rebel forces on these sorties are well armed with automatic rifles, light machine guns, and rocket-launchers.

Only two things seem able to undercut the momentum the resistance has built up during the past year. One would be the fall of the Marxist government itself, highly unlikely, given the extent of the Russian investment. The other would be the strengthening of the Soviet military mechanized land and air forces to overrun the Afghan Revolutionaries. History shows that guerilla movements have an uncanny ability to survive against large conventional armies.

April, 1981
Russians engaged in bitter survival of Afghanistan Moujahedeen
Khot, Afghanistan

The stone frame of a partially completed schoolhouse sits isolated and alone on a hilltop overlooking the Khot River Valley.

The school is one of the hundreds planned by the government of Marxist ideologues in Kabul, hoping to educate socialism to the Afghan people. No one in this province believes the government will return soon to completely finish the school. Even with the help of the Soviet military, it is not strong enough to reassert control.

Nangarhar province is strategically important area along the border with Pakistan, the Russian and Afghan armies are hard pressed by an effective resistance movement, able only to extend themselves to a few urban centers and main roads.

The ease with which Muslim guerillas, who call themselves "Moujahedeen" freedom fighters – move in daylight, heavily armed in flat, open country only a scarce four or five miles from Communist and Afghan garrisons at the provincial capital of Jalalabad is proof of the impotence of the military.

Insurgents, not government employees, hold the keys and operate the pump houses and sluice gates of the American-built Helmand Valley irrigation projects.

The conclusions to be drawn from these observations of the Afghan war is:

Sixteen months after the Soviets occupied Afghanistan to preserve the Marxist revolution and wipe out the armed nationalists is that the freedom fighters are stronger and more confident than ever.

Control of President Karmal, surrogate to the Russians has slowly receded during the same period.

Terrorism – network

The increase assaults on the diplomatic community has brought global attention and national consolidation of countries of peace loving, and sharwo people, what may be their survival in years to come. Isolation of nations that are negligent in providing security for diplomats and embassies, and sanctions against any country that fails to prosecute or extradite criminals, may bring together a community of nations to prevent the Communist intervention any further.

The Lenin Marxist ideology is a serious threat to the world survival to people who want to live in freedom and prosper without state control in their lives.

May, 1981

Terrorism network – Controlled by Red Russia

Approximately 7300 terrorist incidents occurred worldwide during the past 15 years. Over 40% were directed against American citizens or property, mostly overseas. By contrast, few, if any were directed against the Soviet Union or its satellites in Eastern Europe and Africa. The Tass, Soviet Press agency has accused the United States of being "the main center for organizing terrorism," in effect forming groups to attack its own citizens.

In the writings of the Communist leader, V.I. Lenin, as early as 1906, he proposed to his comrades in a clear, brief, concise, and simple plan . . . Supply each group with a clear recipe for making bombs, explain how they work, then leave it up to them. Some may undertake to kill spies, blow up an industrial complex, infiltrate police and security locations, and sabotage their facilities.

The first Russian move in support of international terrorism came after the 1966 Tri-Continental Congress in Havana, Cuba. Emphasis was placed on the need for close collaboration between socialist (Communist) countries and National liberation movements. Ten months later, more than a dozen training camps for terrorists opened in Cuba under Vadim Kochergin of the KGB (Soviet Secret Police). Since then the Lenin ideology has pervaded nearly all of the surrogates of the Marxist states.

Italian terrorism is an expression of an open and legal counterculture as well as an activity of the underground, secret global network. According to Carlo Fioroni, imprisoned for his role in the kidnapping of his closest friend, half the founding leaders of the "Red Brigades" have been trained by the KGB in special camps in Czechoslovakia. A Czechoslovak-manufactured pistol killed the former Prime Minister, "Mors" of Italy.

United States should build up relations with China slowly
Secretary of State, Alexander Haig, in his recent trip to Peking, China, was very dexterous with a touch of diplomatic (Savoir Faire and professional expertise, however the American nation should proceed cautiously in developing open relations with China. It is important to remember that the two countries are fundamentally different societies, but there is a mutual interest in restraining the Soviet Union.

For Washington, China remains an enigma, the Reagan administration is not sure there will not be a turn toward the Kremlin at some point in time. Sober China will be more helpful in maintaining the balance of power, particularly since it cannot become a major military power in this decade.

China is a formidable political and military counterpoint to the Soviet Union, and it is in the United States interest to cooperate with Peking. The Sino-American intelligence is monitoring the Russian missiles from Chinese territory.

The Russian government is neither as strong, nor as weak, as it sometimes appears. It is a closed society marked by low motivation and worker productivity, however it is enmeshed in a stagnant war with Afghanistan and Poland; and is confronted by more than a million Chinese troops on its borders.

July, 1981
Libyan leader Kadaffi manipulates the Organization of African Unity
Nairobi, Kenya

The African heads of state, approximately twenty in number, stayed to the end of the summit meeting of the Organization of African Unity, stated that the Libyans, with their unpredictable leader, Moammar Khadafi, had dominated the conference. In the last year, the government of Libya has sent several thousand troops into one of the provinces, Chad, its neighbor to the South. They broke diplomatic relations with five other African states, bringing to fourteen the number of countries where Libyan diplomats are "persona non grata," not welcome, and has caused wide consternation in all of Africa.

Africa longs to put forward an image of maturity, confidence, and competence – qualities that are becoming visible in some of their nations. It is a continent of fifty separate entities whose governments range within the political spectrum, right to left; radical to reactionary. Some are honest, some are corrupted, with borders artificially imposed and easily inflamed; yet the Organization of African Unity has existed for eighteen years.

The last item of business before the summit closed was the ratification of Tripoli, Libya, as the next summit site.

One of the functions of the Office American Unity is to attempt to mediate disputes between nations when they threaten peace and welfare of the population. How well Khadafi can mediate if his country is one of the parties of the controversy is a question that has to be answered in the future.

Section II

CULTURE AND ENVIRONMENT OF MIDEAST COUNTRIES

Islam-Christianity parallels, foresees the return of Jesus.

Both Moslem and Christian envision "a Second Advent of Jesus Christ," in the world at the end of time. Ushered will be a righteous reign of peace and justice. The concept also resembles Jewish intimations of a longed-for messianic kingdom.

In the midst of earthy chaos, and plunder, Jesus will descend among you as a judge, according to authoritative Islamic tradition, "the Hadith." Not one of the people of the Bible will fail to believe in him. Spite, mutual hatred, and jealousy of one another will certainly depart, and when he summons people to accept wealth, no one will.

In Isaiah 2, it says, "It shall come to pass in the latter days, that the mountain of the house of the Lord shall be established as the highest of mountains. And the people shall flow to it . . . and the Lord alone will be exalted in that day."

In first Corinthians 13:12 of the New Testament, of the Christian Bible: Then shall I understand fully, even as I have been fully understood.

And Sura, chapter of the Koran says, "Then will he, God, show you the truth, of all you did."

That decisive, revealing day, laying bare the self-determined sum of the human lives, in brilliance of full truth, is called the final judgement. Pictures and scriptures of the Jewish, Christian, and Islamic faiths show the world in turmoil until he comes.

Islamic tradition, "hadith," says, "God will send a messenger, the almasih, messiah in Christ. Jesus will seek out and slay the "anti-Christ, called "Dajjal."

Saudi Arabia – is a large kingdom in Southeast Asia. This desert country of mountains, plateaus, and rocky plains, covers two-thirds of the Arabian Peninsula. It is over three times the size of Texas. The capital is Riyadh. About two-thirds of the people are farmers or herdsmen. The farmers raise barley, citrus fruits, dates, wheat, and other crops in oases; fertile areas in desert that have water. The herdsmen are nomads who roam the desert with camels. They have herds of goats, and large groups of sheep.

The country is the birthplace of Islam, a Moslem religion. Mecca and Medina are the chief holy cities. Until the 1930's the Saudi's lived as their ancestors hundreds of years before the emergence of oil well exploration. This brought wealth and new ways of living for the nation. Some of the profits of the oil industry have been used to build new roads, air fields, schools, hospitals, and thriving metropolis to the region recognized as having one quarter of the world's known oil reserve.

Saudi Arabia has four land areas; The Tihama, (Plain), the Western Mountains, the Interior Plateaus, and the Eastern Coastlands. The Tihama lie along a 1200 mile coastline of the Red Sea, and the Gulf of Aquaba. The flat infertile land reaches a width of 40 miles near the city of Juddah. The Western Mountains rise steeply from the Tihama and then slope gently to the east. The

20

jagged red sandstone and black lava peaks of the Hejaz mountain range in the north rise 3000 to 5000 feet near the Gulf of Aquaba. The peaks of the Asir range reach heights of 10,000 feet near the border of the country of Yemen. The Interior Plateaus, almost barren region of sand and rock desert covers nine-tenths of Saudi Arabia. The eastern coastlands lie along a 250 mile Persian Gulf coastline. Gravel or sand is predominant in this rolling plain. Mud flats, lagoons, and sand ridges are specific aerial views.

Petroleum is Saudi Arabia's chief natural resource. The richest deposits are close to the Persian Gulf. There are also traces of gold, silver and copper.

Family life centers on obedience of the Moslem faith. The people pray 5 times a day, and bow toward Mecca at sunrise, noon, mid-afternoon, sunset and nightfall. A man may have as many as four wives; however most can afford to have only one. The women live in one section of the house, the men in another. The rights of females are limited. Boys and girls play together until the age of ten. Then they are separated. Most of the populace are in cities or villages, and they reside in gray, thick-walled houses from two to six stories high. The houses are made of wood frames and sun-dried clay, brick, or stone. High walls surround many of the properties. Following Arab custom, the rooms have no tables or chairs. The individuals sit on pillows, and eat their meals from bowls placed on cloths spread on the floor.

Dates and grain are the primary food supplement. Occasionally meat of sheep, camel, or other animals not of the cloven hoof, are eaten. The men wear baggy trousers and thobs, (loose, ankle-length shirts); Abas, flowing robes of strip camel hair- cloth; over their thobs. They cover their heads with round cotton or wool caps, called Kufiyahs. Over this they wear Gotras, a red or yellow striped cloth held in place by cords or woven wool wrapped around their heads.

The women wear loose trousers under long dresses, called Gomduras, and Haiks, loose veils. Islamic culture requires women to cover their faces in public.

Many of the Saudi Arabian cities are surrounded by walls with tall minarets, towers, and domed mosques; Moslem houses of worship.

The holiest city of this nation is Mecca, the birthplace of Mohammed, founder of Islam. It contains the sacred black stone in the great mosque, called "The Kaaba," worshiped by Moslems. The followers believe their sins will be forgiven if they make a hajj, a pilgrimage to Mecca sometime within their lifetime. The pilgrims march seven times around The Kaaba, kiss the black stone, and participate in religious ceremonies.

The Bedouins, or nomads, roam the countryside with camels, sheep, and goats. Their desert home has little food, or water, and they travel great distances to find grazing land. Each tribe or groups patrol an area. They often go for months eating only dates, cheese, and camel's milk.

The King of Saudi Arabia is the hereditary head of State, and he normally is absolute ruler. He serves as Imam, the religious leader; and his cabinet is titular. As a rule, his brother is Prime Minister, and other members may be family who can serve for an indefinite period. The law is based on the Koran, sacred book of Islam, and on the Sharia, Islamic religious law. Moslems are forbidden to drink alcoholic beverages. Any violation is tried by a citizen council of learned men, Ulema, and presented to the King, to approve or reject the decision.

Mohammed was born in the year 570 A.D. The Caliphs who succeeded Mohammed, formed Arab armies to spread the Islamic faith. In 1945, Saudi Arabia became a charter member of the United Nations, and the Arab League, independent of other states in the region. The national anthem is: "As Salaam al-malaki as Saudi", royal anthem of Saudi Arabia. The basic money unit is the "Riyal."

Syria – Syria is an Arab country at the eastern end of the Mediterranean Sea. It lies at a strategic point on ancient trade routes linking Europe, Asia, and Africa. For thousands of years, Syrians have been famous as merchants and traders, moving goods and services between the three continents. Some of the ancient cities of Damascus, Aleppo, and Palmyra, were found as early as 2000 B.C. The area was a land bridge for caravan routes as well.

Other than trading, the Syrians farm on fertile plains in the Northeast. This land was called, "The Fertile Crescent." The country is about as large as North Dakota. Rolling plains stretch east to the Euphrates River. A desert runs south and west to the Lebanon Mountains. The main waterways are the Orantes River in Lebanon, the Jordan River fed by snows from Mount Hermon, and the Euphrates River passing through the entire nation.

Textiles are the largest single industry. The natives are proficient in their fine leathercraft, brocades, inlaid metalwork, and silver sculpturing. Two pipelines of oil cross the Syrian Desert; one from Iraq, and the other from Saudi Arabia. Transmit fees are the countries major source of income.

The great stretch of grassland and rich soil made Syria a valuable prize, and as a result the nation was a constant battleground, and became part of many empires. The Phoenicians came from the Persian Gulf; the Amorites were the first to settle in the desert; and the Greeks, Moslems, Christians, and Cturks intermingled through centuries of bloody conflict.

Independence for Syria was introduced in 1945, when she and other Arab countries formed the Arab League. As a part of the United Arab Republic, President Assad assembled a government with Arabic as its official language. The national anthem is "Homat el Diyar," Guardians of the Homeland.

Jordan – Jordan is an Arab kingdom in the area of Southwest Asia. The last sandy desert, the rocky plains, and green hills occupies part of the ancient Palestine. Hashemite is a family name of Jordan Kings, and Aman is its capital. Jordan is about the size of Indiana in the United States. Most of the people live in ancient cities and towns that lie close to the Dead Sea and the River Jordan. Some of the communities such as Hebron, Jericho, and Bethlehem are recorded in the Christian Bible.

The country is divided into three main land regions; the Western Uplands, the Rift Valley, and the Eastern Uplands. Bordering Israel is the Western Uplands, steeply rising to the Judean Hills. Samaria is lower, and has wider valleys of rich soil for farming.

The Rift Valley extends south from the Sea of Galilee in Israel to the Gulf of Aquaba. Steep cliffs mostly border the Jordan Valley.

The Eastern Uplands extend from the Rift Valley to heights of more than 4,000 feet slope eastward to the Syrian Desert. The natural resources of this nation have large deposits of bromine and potash in the Dead Sea for exporting out of the country. Jordan also has large deposits of limestone and marble.

Nine out of 10 of the populace are Moslem. The chief cities have modern houses and apartment buildings similar to those of the United States. The people in villages live in flat-roofed houses made of mud-brick. The main diet of the Hashemite is wheat, lamb, vegetables, leban (soured sheep, goat or cow's milk).

Education is free in Jordan. The law requires all children to attend elementary school. The state has a high degree of illiteracy; about three fourths of the individuals cannot read or write.

The Jordanians are highly skilled in the making of jewelry, objects of gold, silver, and copper. Thousands of visitors come to Bethelem, Jericho, and Hebron every year to see the Moslem, Christian, and Jewish holy shrines, and the area where Jesus, the son of God, lived in mortal flesh, and the miracles of healing performed in his presence.

Jordan became an independent state with a treaty signed by Great Britain in 1946. King Hussein, the present ruler of Jordan, assumed the role of supreme commander of the country in 1956. There are nearly two million permanent residents in Jordan now. About 600,000 refugees fled Israel in the Israeli-Arab war in 1948. Most of them live in camps operated by the United Nations. The national anthem is, "Al-Salaam, Al-Malaki," the Royal Salute. The basic money unit is "the Dinar."

Iraq – Iraq is an Arab republic in Southwestern Asia. Baghdad is the capital. The land "of the Arabian Nights," lies on a dry sandy plain between the Tigris and the Euphrates Rivers. It is slightly larger than California in the United States. The people's main diet is rice, dates, mutton, and beef roasted on a skewer, called a "kebab." Most of the Iraqi's drink tea or Turkish coffee. Sheiks, Tribal Chiefs, and the tribesmen live in tents on the sand dunes and gray limestone hills of the Western Desert. The Minarets, Towers, are of the blue, or gold domes of Mosques, Moslem houses of worship. The white-robed Iraqis trade in the narrow, twisting streets, and in crowded bazaars, market places of the major cities.

Profits from Iraq's petroleum have changed the people's way of life. The revenue from the black gold has improved irrigation projects.

Wastelands have been turned into fertile farms. The Greeks call this land Mesopotamia, land between two rivers. Civilizations of Bablonia and Assayria grew and died on the plains. Today only scattered ruins mark the place where these ancient people existed.

Iraq became an independent state in 1964, and they adopted a provisional constitution as a republic, the Head of State a president.

Saddam Hussein is a dictatorial ruler. The country is divided into 14 provinces, called "Liwas." A governor, commissioners, and administrators who complete a governing body lead them. The national anthem is, "Al-Salaam, Al Jumuri," called the anthem of the Republic. Their basic money unit is "the Dinar," worth nearly three dollars in American money.

Kuwait – Kuwait is at the northern end of the Persian Gulf. This desert land is a leading oil producer of the world. This nation is slightly larger than Connecticut in the United States. An undeveloped country until 1946, it is today the richest region in income per person on our globe. She gained her independence from Great Britain in 1961. Islamic faith is predominant. Their constitution forbids any religious, racial or language discrimination.

An Emir, who appoints a Prime Minister, rules the government of Kuwait. A 50-member assembly is the ruling body. The city of Kuwait is its capital, and is near, on the northwest coast of the Persian Gulf. It has good harbors, and serves as a trading center for many cities along the Gulf. Vast oil fields have pipelines for export from the harbors. Fresh water must be imported from neighboring countries.

Lebanon – Lebanon is an independent country in Asia at the eastern end of the Mediterranean Sea. It is nearly the size of Connecticut in the United States. It has been a world trade center for the last 4000 years, and is a gateway between Asia and Europe. The capital is Beirut.

The country is very mountainous, and has a rich history. The cedars of Lebanon have grown on mountain slopes since biblical times. King Solomon obtained this beautiful wood to build his temple in Jerusalem. There are ruins of Phoenician ports, Roman temples, and castles built by the Crusaders still standing.

Lebanon was part of the Ottaman Empire in centuries past. It is considered an Arab country, and Arabic is its official language. More than half of the people are Christian; the rest are Moslem. "The Chamber of Deputies" rules the legislature in Lebanon. The Deputies elect a President to a six-year term. He appoints a Prime Minister and other cabinet officers. The President of this nation must be a Christian of the Maronites; an affiliate of the Roman Catholic Church. The Prime Minister must be a Moslem of the Sunni Sect, an Orthodox.

Neat farm villages stand on mountain slopes. The rugged, hard working farmers wear collarless shirts and baggy trousers, which are tight below the knee. They live in houses of white limestone, with red tile roofs. A wall surrounds their property. The villager meals include Laban, soured yogurt, flat bread, fruit, burgul; crushed whole wheat, lamb, and coffee. More than 80 percent of the populace can read and write.

Lebanon is the financial center of the Middle East. Oil refining is the industrial output for Saudi Arabia, and Persian Gulf crude. The government is Republic. The national anthem theme, "All of Us for Country, Glory, Flag."

12-9-79

Tolerance – Tolerance of world faiths urged by Islamic law. The events taking place in Iran and Syria and Iraq are not justified or sanctioned under the precepts of Islam. Dr. Farouk Abdelwahed, a professor of Cal State Fullerton for Islamic Studies says, "We believe that Jesus, who is a prophet to us, will return to earth on the Day of Judgement. Your Jesus, we call Eisa, and Moses, we call Moussa, will also return."

Mohammed attempted to wipe out idol worship, and to unite the Arabs under a single and pure faith. This was possible only if the Moslems submitted to Allah's will. The Arab for submission is "Islam," and believers are called Muslim, "one who has submitted."

In the beginning, Mohammed was unpopular in Mecca, because most Arabs worshipped many different Gods and Idols. Driven to flight, Hegira, from

Mecca, he found freedom and preached in the City of Yathrib, now called Medina; City of the Prophet. From this base, the Professor said he led military raids against Mecca caravans. This gives rise to the concept of a "Jihad," or Holy War. Mohammed's skill as a military leader attracted many desert tribesmen to his faith, and Mecca soon surrendered to his forces. The man, who was without honor in his own province, re-entered the city in triumph, and extended his empire.

There are five obligations, or pillars of faith. The first duty is profession of faith, proclaiming the oneness of Allah, and acceptance of Mohammed as the Prophet. The second obligation is prayer; at dawn, midday, mid-afternoon, sunset, and nightfall. The Koran describes the required posture, direction toward Mecca, and the language, Arabic.

The only public prayer is at noon each Friday. Attendance by male adults is required. Women may attend, but must stand behind the men.

The third obligation is giving to the poor. In early times, individuals gave from free will, however now taxes are collected and distributed to the needy. The money is used to feed and clothe the poor, and to maintain the mosques.

Fasting, the fourth pillar of Faith, was adapted by Mohammed from Jewish and Christian tradition. It is required during the month of Ramadan, the ninth month of the Muslim calendar. During the 30 days of Ramadan, no food or drink is consumed by the faithful between sunrise and sunset.

The fifth duty is a pilgrimage. Every Muslim, who has the means, must make a journey to the shrine at Mecca before they die. The sacred shrine holds the Kaaba, a black stone preserved by Mohammed.

Human or animal icons are forbidden at Mosques, but Islamic craftsman adorn European and Asian houses of prayer with tiles and carvings of elaborate geometric designs of flowers and trees. Islam is centered on judgement and resurrection.

Unlike the Holy Bible, which was recorded over thousands of years, by many sages and Prophets, and whose revelations are couched in events, the Koran, was produced in a swift 23 years. It is largely extortive. Its appeals and admonitions are molten-hot. Moslems say it is impossible to capture its graphic description of heaven and hell.

While the Koran is the Moslem supreme authority, there are three other sources for it. The Hadith, records personal acts and sayings of Mohammed. The Shiria, gives legal interpretation of the law of its followers. The Ijma, constitutes an additional avenue of decision making.

12-29-79
Lebanon - Shiites versus Sunnis, in the Moslem world

When Moslem fanatics shot their way into the grand Mosque in Mecca, the first reports speculated they were members of the Shia Sect. The often militant Shias who constitute about one tenth of the 800 million Moslems, have become a new reality in the world of Islam, which stretches from Morocco on the Atlantic Ocean, to the Philippines in the Pacific. Members of the Shia majority in Pakistan are believed to have been among the mobs that attacked the United States Embassy, spreading rumors that Americans were responsible for the seizure of the holiest shrine in Mecca, Saudi Arabia. Turkey, a member of the North Atlantic Treaty

Organization, has a substantial number of Shiites in its eastern providence, and bloody battles have occurred between the Sunnis and the militant Shias.

The nature of Shiism contains strong elements for developing political power. The Sunnis do not have a formal clergy, on the grounds it would create an intermediary between the believer, one who submits, and Allah. The Shias have a structured clergy; the low level Mullahs, an equivalent of a parish priest, and the higher ayatollahs and Imams, who are nearer to Allah, the Moslem God. The Shias are given to Martydom, to defy the whole world. In their mind, there is no compromise.

11-25-79
Moslem Women

For many women, the Anachristic way of life, in which their marriage is arranged, they now are allowed to participate in the bridal selection of their mate, in which their romance can flourish and grow. The families of the Moslems are very close. Brothers, sisters and cousins can mingle and play together. One of the family members is chosen for a young bride. The restrictions placed on her are as simple as narrowing the field. She can choose from a selection of possible male suitors. The Moslems do not want the bride to be forced into an unwanted relationship.

A young man of Islamic faith was asked how he viewed the restrictions for marriage, and he said, "My mother was the lady of our house. She had nothing to do but execute what her husband told her. She did not eat her meals with him, but after. She did not call her mate by his first name. I would imitate she was like a piece of furniture you take care of. She did not see much of the outside world. She is a devout Muslim, praying five times a day, and quotes from the Koran."

The young Muslim was born in a village on the Nile River Delta, and grew up in a middle class family of eleven children. He lives and works in Cairo, Egypt. His father is not so religious. He believes in God, Allah, and is a loyal farmer who provides well for his family, however, he looks at women as a second-rate human beings. From my background, our women have gained in prestige and individuality. Some are working or going to school, working as journalists, but the majority is reigned to being a wife and mother. Islam is a system that has affected the way of life of the Moslem, and there are inbred values that are difficult to escape from.

12-8-79
Libya – Era of the masses predicted by Moamar Khadafi

The iron fisted Moslem ruler of Libya believes anti-United States actions in Iran and his own country are the beginning of an international revolution against the American State, and the world is aware of what he has preached for a decade, "The era of the masses." The Moslem ruler, who has no government title, allowed a fanatical mob to ransack the U.S. Embassy in Tripoli, Libya's capital.

The North African desert is mostly Arab Moslems, and is one of the largest oil producers of the region. Khadafi has aligned his country with the hard-lined Arab States that oppose the Egyptian-Israeli peace treaty. According to the rejectionist leader, Jamahiriah, which means democracy, is ruled by people without parties, parliaments, or governments. It calls for the future destiny to be worldwide.

An Italian colony from 1912 to World War II, Libya became an independent state in 1951. It grew anti-western before Khadafi seized power in 1969. One of his first actions was to close down the United States and British military bases. He nationalized the oil companies, and his fixation is to end Israel as a Jewish state through repatriation of European Jews back to their countries of origin. This movement will return the Palestinians to their usurped land added Khadafi.

1979
Iran – A letter from a concerned clergy to Khomeini

When a letter from Ayatollah Khomeini was published in the New York Times in November 1979, the American ministers responded as follows: "The clergy, priests, and monks who invite the souls of the unruly to calmness, by the teachings of Jesus Christ."

We speak to the inconsistencies between the spoken word and his actions. Less than a year ago, Khomeini preached justice, equality, peace and compassion. You gave the impression that your role in this government would be that of an advisor. In the same breath, you stated that you would be "the strong man" of Iran. The image is clear to us that you are an egomaniac, not a holy man of peace. You are not a reconciliator, but a picture of a man of vengeance, hiding under a clerical robe.

You do not intend to release the innocent Americans you hold as hostage, even though the Vienna Convention on Diplomatic Relations guarantees the independence and sovereignty of embassies in foreign lands. You preach the faithful adherence to Islamic law, yet act against the directives of the Shiria, Islamic Cannon law. It specifically states and orders the protection of emissaries and envoys. You claim the name of God as merciful and compassionate, yet you kill without mercy, and use American pawns for your own manipulation and goals. The secret trails and executions that you have conducted against those who disagree with you demonstrate your contempt for the traditions and cannons of Islamic faith.

Chapter Two

Other Lands and Other People

12-29-79
Invasion of Afghanistan by the Soviet Union has suddenly catapulted this highly important country into a world conscious of imbalance of power. It is a disregard of the sovereignty of an independent nation. What happens in Afghanistan may shape the future of the entire Asian hemisphere.

The brutal occupation of the country, and the largest troop movement by Moscow since World War II, and the breakup of détente is a mockery of international justice. Afghanistan is a land-locked nation about the size of Texas in the United States, bound on the north by the USSR, on the west by Iran; on the south by Pakistan, and on the extreme northeast by the people's republic of China.

The populace is fiercely independent. They have not permitted foreign domination for any length of time. There are hundreds of small villages here headed by a clan called a Malik, and nominated by elders. The people have tiny plots of privately held land, or work as tenants for a local landowner. The classic act of imperialism presents serious problems. Troop movement is a direct threat to Pakistan and Iran. It is less than 500 miles to the Arabian Sea where Soviet aircraft could interfere with American naval forces. Detachments of Moslem forces have turned their guns on the new enemy, referred to as "the invaders."

In the capital of Jalalabad, east of Kabul, the national Afghan Army, with Muslim guerilla groups, is opposing the Soviet vanguard. Although poorly trained, historically the Afghanis are amazing antagonists, when once they take up arms. They will fight to the finish. Weather has been a factor, with snow and ice slowing the progress of the communist insurgents.

The Russians can be expected to drive deeper into the vital Persian Gulf oil regions to claim a warm water series of harbors.

Pakistan – Pakistan and the Middle East threatened by Russian Hegemony
The Soviet invasion of Afghanistan has caused distress in many of the capitals of the world, but nowhere more than in Pakistan. It has felt the only real ally is the United States. The Moslem country wants not only arms from the Americans, but a show of support that may include permanent bases to counter attack the Russian military mechanized divisions and air protection.

In the interest of national security, the Carter Administration can resume military assistance despite the restrictions. Aircraft and armored vehicles and spare parts are vital to rebuff an attack from outside forces. The Soviet Union is clever, extolling hegemony, political domination, as an introduction to an aggressive takeover of a sovereign nation that interferes with the communist politburo. Muslim unity is a hazard to Marxist Ideology, and the holy war of Jihad, may imperil the communist existence.

The Russians moved quickly into the Vietnam vacuum, shouldering aside the Chinese, who struggled briefly for position. The Kremlin dispatched Cuban troops to the Portuguese colony of Angola, and established a beachhead in Africa. Naked aggression suppressed a revolt by the black militiamen in 1977, and the Russians installed a Marxist regime.

28

The communists will exploit any weakness outside the Soviet sphere of operations. They would rather gain control of a satellite through subversion, other than a direct aggressive military invasion. The strategy in lower Asia of the Soviets calls for the dismemberment of Afghanistan, Pakistan and Iran into separate ethnic states. Then the Russian communists will envelop the territory by subversion and diabolical agreements of unification and protection. It is a sobering assessment. The paralyzing effect would give the Marxist nation frontage on both the Persian Gulf and the Indian Ocean.

Yemen – Soviet Marxist moving to envelop all of Yemen

With the attention of American policy makers focused on armed conquest by the Soviet Union in Afghanistan, the Russians are diplomatically engaged in the Middle East area of Yemen. It is a region menacing close to the American source of oil.

Events in recent months suggest that North Yemen, which borders Saudi Arabia on the south, and guards the entrance to the Red Sea and the Suez Canal is leaning in the direction of the communist bloc, contrary to western influence. The regime of Abdullah Saleh, is apparently willing to defy convention and proceed with the unification with South Yemen. This is a sensitive situation, as South Yemen has become a principal training camp for terrorist groups. The two Yemens completed a round of talks, focusing on organizing legislative and executive powers, a transition toward building a unified central state.

This would place about seven million Yeminis near the border of Saudi Arabia, who currently employ over one million Yeminis in the Arabian oil fields. In addition to closer ties with Moscow, the entrance to the Red Sea can be controlled by having communist outposts on both sides of the strategic waterway to the Suez. Ethiopia has 20,000 crack Cuban troops for military combat. The western nations should observe and scrutinize the actions taken in this sector of the world.

The visible evidence of the soviets toward the Persian Gulf terrifies the Arabian states of Syria, Saudi Arabia, Iraq, and the Gulf Emirates. If the communists replace the American strength and prestige, it will increase the vulnerability of leftist coups in the Middle East. Americans should promptly establish its military competence to cope with further Soviet penetration surrounding the Gulf. A permanent task force in the Indian Ocean is a step.

1-29-80

Yugoslavia – Russian imperialism may spread to include Yugoslavia

The current Soviet involvement in Afghanistan has sent a chill into Yugoslavia's ruling circles. With the instability of the President, Marshall Tito, having surgery on his ailing leg, the countries ruling pro-Communists may decide this is the time to seize the Marxist State.

To his credit, Tito has brought his faction-ridden nation a degree of prosperity unknown in the eastern bloc. Likewise, the system has allowed limited economic and political freedom, both of which serves as escape valves for the 22 million citizens. The six ethnic republics compromise the Yugoslav federal state. Because of his split with the Soviet Union, the president has been regarded as a socialist bridge between the east and the west. His non-aligned movement has brought about a third world status to power restricted nations.

Military strength is the hallmark of Tito for armed preparedness. There are 250,000 men in service with over half a million reserves. The territorial defense force is a large citizen army, and directly controls the federal republics.

The Kremlin has viewed any opposition to Yugoslavia, communist or not, as threatening the Warsaw's southern flank. As long as they are not entangled with internal crises, there will be no pressure from the Moscow émigrés.

National tensions in the Soviet Union would exert pressure on the satellites. Bulgaria would be fired up to enter Macedonia; pro-western ethics in Slovenia and Croatia might be encouraged to seek separation from the communist bloc; and other communist states may seek assistance from the NATO Alliance as an independent state.

Africa – Somalia offers the United States a military base
Barring any unforeseen circumstances, Washington will complete an agreement, giving the United States use of military facilities at Berbera, the former Russian naval and airbase on the Gulf of Aden in East Africa.

Berbera, a hot, barren, arid city of 20,000 people has a base near a mountain range, 160 miles across from a Soviet stronghold at Aden, South Yemen, on the Arabian Peninsula. The Berbera airfield has a 15,000 foot runway long enough to accommodate transport planes and B-52 Bombers. There is space for repair shops, tenders, warehouse for storage, and tanks for aviation and ship fuel.

The Americans are seeking long-termed facilities in Somalia, Kenya, and Oman, to bolster its ability to respond militarily to communist threats in the Persian Gulf and Indian Ocean. Expansion of the American base on Diego Garcia Island and deployment of an aircraft carrier task force is strengthening the power structure of the western nation.

The United States has had no permanent presence in black Africa since it was expelled from Kagnew, a communications region in Asmara, Ethiopia in 1977. In Mombassa, Kenya, the Americans will have continued access in any international crisis.

The program will position military equipment and supplies to be used in emergencies and rapid response forces that can be sent by air or sea lift.

The western country can proceed with the buildup carefully, to minimize disruption of the natives, and their way of life. Somalia is extending their friendship and cooperation to us.

Afghanistan – Moslems in Afghanistan demand independence
In Barogai, Afthanistan, Asif Sayeed is a rebel. He calls himself Mujahid, or Holy War Fighter. Sayeed lives in a mud and rock grotto in a tiny village with strategic importance disproportionate to its size. The village is located in Kunar Province, in eastern Afghanistan. A rebellion began more than two years ago, and the region overlooks Chigha Sarai, the capital of Kunar. Also, nearby is Kerala, a town where many of its male residents were massacred by government troops in April 1979.

To Sayeed, it is a Jihad, or Holy War, and included in this sharp reaction is the tampering of customs and the independence of their tribal life. The invasion of Russian forces makes the rebels angry, and although greatly outnumbered in men and equipment, fights fiercely, and they know the terrain. The Afghans are determined to resist, and the tribal leader says, "We will be the first nation to throw out communism. We are not counting the years, however, as long as the Soviets are here, we will fight."

The Soviet invasion of Afghanistan was strategically timed. It came after the affair of the American hostages. The United States not only lacked diplomatic and military clout for their release from illegal seizure by the Iranian students, but was also powerless to prevent subjugation of a neighboring country.

In 1919, on the eve of the Versailles Peace Conference, and establishment of the League of Nations, the newly born Soviet Union declared war on its neighbor, Finland, and annexed part of its territory. In 1940, the Russians annexed three small individual Baltic States, Latvia, Estonia, and Lithuania. Without a gun being shot. The Western possession of superior military might has not, in itself prevented Soviet expansion.

2-25-80
Zambia – Communist governed Zambia purchases Soviet military equipment
A reporter from Johannesburg, South Africa confirms that Zambia has purchased 85 million dollars worth of Soviet military arms, including supersonic Mig-21 jets. This reflects the interest of Russia in South Africa.

Diplomatic sources said the package involves armored cars and personnel carriers, as well as Soviet built tanks. Zambians are undergoing training in the Russian nation to maintain and use the weapons. The President of Zambia, Kaunda, wants to bolster his forces from potential enemies, but unlike its agreements with Mozambique and Angola, the Soviet Union is requiring 20 percent cash down, and the rest over a seven year period.

The arms purchase can push Zambia closer to independence of the Marxist State, and rely on good will for spare parts, technical advisors and specialists to service the Mig-21's and other military hardware.

According to British dignitaries, there are over 45,000 Cuban Communists in Africa. Thirty-five thousand of them are soldiers, and the others technicians.

The Russians have spread their Communism through ideology, in addition to making friends with people on different levels, and in support of African nations with disputes concerning the United States. Hundreds of Soviet Union grants of scholarships each year are handed out to individuals meeting standards for Russian institutions, through the Communist party offices.

Entrenchment also exists in South Africa and the People's Republic of China.

Argentina – South America and Central America are targets of Russian acceptance.
In Buenos Aires, Argentina, the Soviet Union is making a skillful effort to expand its importance in what one writer describes as "America's strategic retrenchment." The Russian progress has been gradual, gaining momentum and disregarding setbacks in certain areas of the Southern Hemisphere.

The Soviet embassy in Argentina is centered in the capital's most influential neighborhood, with diplomas speaking Spanish fluently, and learning the political and cultural history of the society. The Russians are aimed for every ability and intelligence level, using performing artists, the Moscow Circus, classical musicians and dancers to engender themselves into the hearts of the people.

The Soviet Union wants and needs grain for their populace and would like to have access to the abundant fishing grounds in the Atlantic coastal waters. In addition, Russia would appeal to the leaders to arrange a contract to sell arms to all the Latin American countries. Also the Kremlin could profit by establishing landing rights for their airline, Aeroflot.

China – China sees Russian Hegemony as global imperialism
The dissonant views of China and the Soviet Union became apparent in the early 1960's. The Premier of Russia then, Nikita Khrushchev, withdrew a division of technicians from the Chinese nation, with blueprints of all the factories they were constructing, and before the year was out, a battle of wills ensued. The rift grows wider each day, and the chasm grows deeper and wider, with no communication between them. Official sources confirm the Russian vanguard continues to march. They register no feeling or consider a country's right, only to suppress.

Cuba – Fidel Castro is a Russian puppet. While he speaks on a universal stage of non-aligned nations, he has transformed Cuba into a Russian colony, dependent on a subservient to Moscow. The relentless reds, in turn, are using Cuba as a military base, in flagrant violation of the Monroe Doctrine.

The Cuban President has vowed, "Never has the Soviet Union, which as given such decisive aid to our citizens, approached us to demand favors. They have not set forth conditions," however, intelligence reports have shown that Castro listens and follows directives of the Politburo. The brash Cuban member of the Soviet team says bilateral relations have never been better.

The Latin American President has refrained from intervention in the American territory directly, but he supports insurgents. In Guatemala and El Salvador, he destabilizes, then subverts the countries by revolution. The Soviets want field bases to strike the United States when the time is ripe.

In Cuba, red fighter planes, combat troops disguised as technicians, and reconnaissance aircraft patrol the coastlines. Submarine and intelligence operations are active, and the Soviet Union is planning construction of nuclear warheads to combat the missiles projected by the Western and NATO powers.

By contrast, the American war with Vietnam lasted for more than 13 years, the salt 2 negotiations have been in effect for more than 10 years, and the Arab-Israeli conflict lasted more than 30 years before the signing of the Camp David Accords for Peace. Despite several wars and many crises, the Americans are limited in scope and change. Dynamic forces can accelerate the course of history. Re-evaluating the commitment of the western super power, they should polarize plans with their allies, enforce an international security and prevent domination of any nation or group of nations.

Austria – In Vienna, Austria, Bruno Kreisky, the Chancellor of Austria, States that the pullout of the Soviet troops from Afghanistan is not possible at this time. Until the Kremlin has solved its problems of leadership, brought on by the infirmity of President Leonid Brezhnev, the communists will use the intervention as a deterrent of aggression. Kreisky has survived many clashes of internal strife, and diplomatically led his party in triumph over German and Russian interference.

32

According to Kreisky, the Soviets are flexible, and neutrality for Afghanistan may be a part of a general policy to strengthen their relations with the western nations. They may limit nuclear and conventional arms also.

With the attention of the Islamic world focused on the Afghan crisis, the communists may try to intervene in the Arab-Israeli discussion, and suggest the Palestinians seek self-determination or a separate State.

In another sector of the Asian world, the President of Lebanon, Elias Sarkis, declares support for a Palestinian homeland, but rejects a permanent settlement on Lebanese soil. In addition, Sarkis intimates, an established state must have the legal resources alone, without the presence of armed groups. Russia views this situation as a lever for developing friendly relations for communist expansion.

3-5-80

Universal – A fragile balance of power exists in the international order. Recent attacks on the American Embassy are omens of a deeper division in the community of nations. Like seismic tremors, or the signal of an earthquake, public apathy seems to follow.

The shift in the east-west balance of power has occurred gradually, as has the expansion of the Soviet Union geopolitical influence. Some twenty years ago, the United States enjoyed vast reserves of military and governmental prestige, but the impact is shrinking universally. Referring to history, in the 1950's, the United States maintained a base in Libya, and military facilities in Ethiopia. Now, the Soviet surrogates are firmly entrenched. Our British allies had a naval base in Aden Arabia and Singapore, while today the Russian fleet is harbored in Cam Ranh Bay supplying Vietnam.

Because of this erosion in geographic assets, the west capability to cope with a crisis is becoming weaker. Each future setback is dangerous, tilting the balance of power.

Napoleon Bonaparte completed the expansion of his giant empire from Spain to Russia within some 17 years, in an era when communications and travel were immeasurably slower than the present. Hitler's achievement, the collapse of a collective security system of the League of Nations, rearmament of Germany, and annexing of territories, which eventually lead to a world war; all of these events took place in a span of 13 years.

We should condemn the conduct of the Communist leaders, not the country. In political costs, we should maximize the pain and suffering by restrictions of technology transfers, wheat sales, and diplomatic contacts. The suffering of international prestige will do more to destroy their image than any other single penalty, and in the eyes of bilateral country's, lose confidence.

Moscow, Russia – The current struggle in Afghanistan is not the first time the Kremlin has waged against Muslim rebels bent on preserving their way of life. There was a similar clash in the years following the 1917 Revolution that brought the Communists to power. The Bolsheviks under Lenin were moving to consolidate Soviet rule over Central Asia who had been subjugated by the Czars of Russia.

Some experienced diplomats concede the Kremlin is using the same tactics today, and throughout the Islamic world. The Basmachi rebellion, the oppressed, erupted in the region of the Caspian Sea, east of the frontier of China and Mongolia. The rebels were disorganized and ill equipped, but their guerilla tactics were effective. They kept the Red Army on the run for more than a decade. They were made up of Partisan detachments, almost exclusively on horseback. They were elusive, and often dissolved into neighboring villages, literally before the eyes of the Soviet troops.

In the end, the Baschi rebellion was crushed, with brutal force, combined with periodic concessions to national customs that masked, but did not alter their goal: of undermining the Islamic foundation.

The Basmachi movement did not attain its ultimate purpose, to overthrow the Russian rule in Turkestan, because the Reds were better organized, and had at their disposal more experienced military. What is required now is unification of Moslems with the aim to protect their people and property from invaders, wherever they are.

In the meantime, Prime Minister Menachem Begin of Israel has offered military bases to the United States. Begin stated, "If the Americans want facilities in our country, they shall have them."

The Prime Minister declared that in the light of the hostage crisis in Iran, and the Soviet invasion of Afghanistan, the U.S. must have access.

Oman – In Muscat, Oman, the United States has completed the first phase of negotiations toward a new military alliance that will allow the North American nation to use bases near the Persian Gulf in exchange for a commitment to defend them.

The two countries have reached a basic agreement on a pact that will give the American Air Force access to three Omani air bases, one of them 240 miles from the Straight of Hormuz. The Navy will be granted facilities at Oman's two ports. In return, the Western nation will pay for improvements to the air and naval bases, supplying the armed forces of Oman with new weaponry, and a pledge to defend the Arab principality in event of an alien attack.

The United States Navy Task Force patrols the waters south of Iran, and is presently using Oman for re-supply. Small airplanes from the aircraft carriers Nimitz and the Coral Sea fly in and out of the city of Muscat ferrying mail and perishables. The Carter Administration would like to develop a rapid deployment attack division in the region with over 20,000 men.

The government of Oman has asked Washington for anti-tank missiles, C-130 transport planes, anti aircraft radar and missile systems, gunboat and mine sweepers to patrol the Straight of Hormuz for defense purposes.

Omani Information Officer, Abdul Rawwas inducates, "With the Russians in the Horn of Africa, in South Yemen, and in Afghanistan, we are seeing the expansion of a colonial power." Under the terms of a 20 year friendship agreement, signed last October between Moscow and Aden, Arabia, the Kremlin has brought surveillance jets to the region, developed dry dock facilities to service up to 12 submarines at one time, and can house and support several thousand men.

4-5-80
Iraq – In Baghdad, Iraq, Saddam Hussein is the strongman. Critics, mindful of the enemies he has executed by the score, call him the butcher of Baghdad. Supporters say, that more than any other Arab leader, he eschews visionary goals. He is stereotyped, "the Engineer of Revolution." He is the fulcrum of the

Middle East melting pot of confusion. A reputation as a revolutionary has given Hussein an opening to the progressive regimes in Syria, Libya, South Yemen, and Algeria. A strong army, and commandos for hire, put him in position to threaten, and protect for a price; Saudi Arabia, Kuwait, and the weaker sheikdoms of the Persian Gulf.

In Baghdad, in 1978, at a summit meeting, most of the nations of the Arab League joined Iraq in condemning Egyptian President Anwar Sadat's separate peace treaty with Israel. In March of 1980, Saddam issued an eight-point charter, designed to hold Russia and the United States out of the Persian Gulf, while casting Iraq in a leading role as a supreme protector of the region.

In Tripoli, in April 1980, at a conference, the Syrian President, Assad, met with other radical heads of State from Libya, Algeria, South Yemen, and the Palestine Liberation Organization, to affirm the strongest possible stance against the Egyptian-Israeli Peace Accords.

This action, by Arab Revolutionaries results in a three-way split in the Moslem world; Sadat, moving toward a settlement with Israel under American auspices; Hussein, pushing for the non-aligned Arab nations, and the radicals, led by Syria's Assad, supported by the Kremlin of the Soviet Union.

6-4-80

The superpowers are keenly aware of nuclear arms annihilation. Military force is clearly a major reality, but three factors inhibit its use by the United States and the Soviet Union, in the present post-Afghanistan era: the worldwide availability of modern weapons; the volatile nationalism; and the irrelevance of combat in international situations.

There are five acknowledged nuclear weapons states. India has exploded a nuclear device; Israel and South Africa are questionable; potential new members of the nuclear club are mainly to be found in the third world. Guerillas, saboteurs, and terrorists can paralyze and impede invading armies.

Nationalism represents a powerful deterrent, as Washington has discovered in Vietnam, and Moscow is learning in Afghanistan. A country with ideals and fierce determination will resist foreign domination. Also subversion by the Russians of a free nation has alienated the non-aligned countries, enraged the Moslems, and antagonized the western superpower.

In most events the use of military might is irrelevant:
- The United States could not use it to free the hostages in Iran.
- The Reds did not prevent China from invading Vietnam.
- The Peace Treaty between Japan and China was not blocked.
- Pope John Paul of the Vatican was able to reach the Polish faithful, in which millions of people renounced the Atheists of the Kremlin, yielding to a higher power, God.

If peace on our globe is to continue, a balance of power must be maintained. A way to keep this balance is to plan, develop and work for harmony by exchanging technology and automation. Concentrate on space and medical breakthroughs in future experiments.

Arabs pressure Oman to bring about Moslem unity. The Sultan of Oman, Kaboos Ibn Saud, is an American ally on the Persian Gulf, and has been the odd man out in the Arab region. It is the one country on the Arabian Peninsula ready to accept the western military, and the only country to support Egypt in the Peace Treaty. They have absolutely no relations with the Palestinian Liberation Organization.

The United States is negotiating a pact with the sultanate at the precise moment his nation is moving closer to its Arab cousins. The Omanis practice a separate kind of Islam. They remain adherents to the Ibadhi Sect, described as, "Quakers of Islam," Bereft of a Clergy.

The United Arab Emirates has financed roads across the Omani Desert, with a clear means of travel from Muscat to Abu Dhabi. Their television satellite communication and technology reaches the far corners of the world.

Demands from the Palestinians may cause the Sultan to quietly withdraw his support of the Camp David Accords. As a first step toward a comprehensive settlement, including Palestinian autonomy, Oman concurred it is a good plan, but should it fail, the people of Oman would pressure Kaboos Ibn Saud to rejoin the Moslem rejectionists.

Monarchies are unlikely to be bedfellows to Baghdad's radical socialists, however the forces of evil never give up. The nations of the Mideast must be constantly on the alert against any invasion.

In another sector of the Middle East and Asia, are the Baluchis, credited with being the "Sentinels of the Straight of Hormuz." One of the least known wars in modern history ended in 1977, in the hills and valleys of Southwestern Pakistan.

The war pitted the Pakistan Army against an indomitable tribe of people.

1-6-82
Poland – When Poland's military chiefs declared martial law last December 1981, security forces and militia rounded up more than 6,000 national, regional and factory level leaders of the Independent Trade Union, Solidarity.

Information reaching Washington D.C. indicated they are kept in camps, prisons, and vacation resorts. From a diary that was smuggled out of an internment camp is a pronouncement of the seizure of a Polish resistance movement. Arrest warrants were issued on December 12, to the controlling forces with automatic weapons and long rubber truncheons. Individuals were led into dark passageways to cold, confined rooms with tiny barred windows that were slightly opened. In the room was a platform, with bare boards. The cells exceeded the worst fears of the internees. The dimensions were 8x10 feet, with three iron bunks. Next to them a stopped up toilet. The windowpanes were broken and the rooms unheated, with torn, dirty mattresses. The cold was chilling, and made the nights unbearable. The morning meals consisted of rotten potatoes, with saltwater soup.

It was hard to tolerate the cell, added the informer. The commandant informed those arrested that a State of War was proclaimed in Poland, and no international law applied to them, and the prisoners were deprived of all rights.

Liquidation of Solidarity was started. Union members, still at liberty, were given two alternatives; resign from Solidarity, or lose their jobs. The Union's full time leaders were given no work, no unemployment benefits, and were condemned to starve. Under the hard conditions of persecution by the regime, human ties in the Polish society were strengthened. The efforts to atomize the nation produced an opposite effect. Freedom now, they said.

7-4-82
Lebanon
What does the future hold for Lebanon? Israel considers that intervening in the affairs of the Middle East country will bring relief for the Israelis along the borders of Syria and Lebanon from the Palestinian Liberation Organization terrorizing its people.

When the Israeli tanks rolled across the Lebanese frontier in June 1982, Prime Minister Menachem Begin announced that their objective was to free the Jewish populace from tactics of sabotage and slow annihilation. Except for some cables of encouragement, the Kremlin in Russia abandoned the Palestinians in their hour of crisis. They set back while Israel destroyed Syria's Soviet-made air defense system. The Red Proletariat continues to exclude itself from any Mideast peace process, especially, "The Camp David Accords."

No nation will leave the war in Lebanon with clean hands. The Arab countries give nothing but lip service. The nationalists in Lebanon have suffered huge losses in human life, and have lain waste the largest trade cities in the Mediterranean.

What the Israeli invasion has created is a successful Arab summit in Fez Morocco, whose leaders have rose above their purblind thinking of the past to accept reality of the Jewish State in the Middle East. Two factors have given the Moroccan meeting special significance: Politically, the Moslems have moved to counter the strategy for autonomy of the Palestinians on the West Bank and Gaza Strip, by calling for a separate land for peace stance. The second reason vital to the Fez Summit is psychological. The Moslems, thoroughly rejecting, and disproving the treaty of Egypt and Israel have claimed the country non-existent. The history dates back to when the British presented the White Paper to the Palestinians in 1948, offering them an independent State in ten years, restricting the Jewish State's land purchase from Arabs.

Soviet Union
Brezhnev, Dictator of the Soviet Union dies. The Bear of Russia is dead. Leonid Ilyich Brezhnev passed away on November 10, 1982 at the age of 75, and has bequeathed to the Red Communist nation a Pandora's Box of problems: A Moribund agriculture, a static industrial empire, a passive Communist party, and a monumental task of maintaining strategic parity with the United States.

Many of his colleagues saw him as a dogged bureaucrat, who never deviated from predictable norms; who played by the rules, and did not let his predecessor, Nikita S. Krushchev, convince him to deliberately defy the decisions of the Politburo, which led to his overthrow.

Many of the countrymen of Russia fear that the successor, Yuri Andropov, will not help their economy. The former head of the Communist secret police has been promptly and decisively picked by the eleven-manned Politburo to lead the Soviet Union. There is fear by some intellectuals that Andropov might move as a Stalinist, with internal repressions, mass arrests, and a new empire of prison camps.

Brezhnev had been head of the Soviet Union for over 18 years, from October 1964, when Krushchev was removed from office. The Politburo developed a "stability of the Cadres," a lifetime tenure on the job to all the high party officials. The problem that confronts Russia is old men directing other old men. Younger enthusiasts have been held to inferior positions, and have to wait for the elders to die, or be overthrown.

The stakes in the post-Brezhnev era are very high. In reality, the Americans can benefit from relaxation of the arms race, and return to cooperation in technology, where sharing would lessen tension between the super powers. Once a Soviet leader dies, the new leadership will be tested. There is reason to believe Andropov is moving swiftly to demonstrate his power.

Soviet Union

Without the backing of the military chiefs, the bosses of big urban industrial party organizations, and the secret police, which he has long supervised, Andropov would not have smoothly taken over as General Secretary, however his opponents lurk in the shadows.

As for Foreign Policy, the President of the Soviet Union may prove willing to compromise if the United States is ready to match any concessions. With the economy, Andropov may alter the hard-line of his predecessor. Decentralizing may come easy for him. His expertise in Hungary where he was Ambassador during the 1956 uprising, and his dealings with the Eastern European countries may convince the Politburo that reforms in the Soviet Union can be useful. Hungary's economic system, which allows some free enterprise, is the healthiest of the Communist bloc.

Face saving in Afghanistan is more difficult. They have sent an estimated 100,000 troops to crush the Moslem populace, and have gained very little. As for Poland, Soviet ideology will not tolerate Solidarity without government control.

Only time can tell if the free world and the Communists will join in peaceful pursuit for a civilized society.

President Tito of Yugoslavia, for many years ruled their country with an iron hand. He imposed not a solution, but static movement upon problems with a people with hostile tradition; coexisting. His argument was simply to survive. The nation of Communist sympathizers remained party oriented, but federally controlled. His republics assumed major powers, for the economic progress, with mutual dependence of the nationalities, and practices of a non-aligned foreign policy. Because power is delegated, every major item that comes before the federation requires a consensus. The assembly gives final decisions.

Section III
Ukraine – Also affected is the rest of Europe, and even the United States
The very borders between Russia and the Ukraine in addition must be agreed on.
Gorbachev and several Russian leaders warned Kravchuk that Russia might seek
to reclaim major areas such as the Crimea, and the Industrial region around
Kharkov, that were given to the Ukraine by the Kremlin. Kravchuk declared
emphatically that the Ukraine has become an Independent state by the will of the
people.

All this leads some Soviet officials to speculate that after months of
posturing, then negotiating, the Ukraine will agree to participate in a loose
confederation, but with veto power for every member, not just Russia.
December 3, 1991
Independence for the Ukraine
A reporter in the Soviet Union indicated the Ukranian people have voted
overwhelmingly for Independence from the Soviet Union, breaking with decades
of failed Socialism and centuries of Russian domination. This is a priority for their
newborn nation.

Ukranian President Elect M. Kravchuk, chosen to lead his republic to
independence, will be trying to reshape the relationship that many of his people
believed they are voting on to end, a close coordination of policies with Russia,
the perennial "Big Brother." Hard realities give him and his people little choice.

Even a country larger than France, and nearly as populace, remains a
prisoner of its geography and history. Just as the Ukraine's participation
reconstitutes the country as a confederate state its decision to seek full
independence will affect the course of the other republics. Russian President
Boris N. Yeltsin, has warned other republic leaders here last week that until the
Ukraine inks the political treaty, Russia will not sign it either. Russia does not
intend, Yeltsin made it clear, to be maneuvered into a Union with the
impoverished Republics of Soviet Central Asia, so that Mikhail S. Gorbachev can
continue to preside over a central government while Russian wealth is drained
away.

Let the Ukraine be "free as the wind" and pursue a course it chooses,
Yeltsin said, as he told the other dignitaries, however we will have to respond
accordingly, not to be taken unawares.

As a new military power in Europe, with a nuclear arsenal larger than
that of Great Britain or France, and with plans for an army bigger than that of
Germany, the Ukraine will need to quickly declare its adherence to the major arms
control accords or risk confrontation with Russia.
Commonwealth Formed with Slavic States
It is reported that President Boris Yeltsin, with the leaders of the Ukraine and
Belarus, on December 8, declared the Soviet Union as a super power dead, and
established a new "commonwealth" of independent states, with the capital in
Minsk, which is the capital of Belarus today, instead of Moscow.

V.I. Lenin created the continent-size state of the Soviet Union, 69 years ago, which came to be a vanguard of Communist resolution across the globe, the greatest power in Europe, and the chief cold war threat to the United States.

A statement from the coalition pledges that the members will coordinate their economic reforms, jointly control nuclear weapons, and adhere to the international agreements of the former Soviet Union. Other states sharing the aims and principles of the new union are welcome to be part of the commonwealth.

Gorbachev still holds his place in history, as the man who started the dramatic reform program that destroyed the dictatorship of the Communist Party in his own country. He sparked the Democratic people's revolution in Eastern Europe and ended the Cold War.

Waiting in the wings, in Moscow, is Boris Yeltsin's enemies, the Soviet Communist Regime, the only organized force opposing Yeltsin and his policies from Anarchists to Monarchists.

A conservative movement will be formed by early January, if the present Russian government is swept away by an angry populace. Volodin, a political commentator of a Soviet newspaper, indicates their future is stark; riots are soon to begin, with hungry mobs on the rampage. The apocalyptic view is the President of Russia's reforms has already been defeated before they start in earnest.

Commonwealth Formed

Volodin added that in no more than three months, we would have brief periods of strikes, and street demonstrations. Removing price support controls amid monopolized production is suicidal. There will be a tidal wave of crime, both against institutions and individuals, and then the military will step in.

With memories of a failed coup last August still fresh, a neo-conservative, Tatiana I. Koryagina, insisted they are anxious not to give the impression they are plotting another takeover. It won't be a "putsch," an up rising, she added.

Is Mikhail Gorbachev a man without a country? For more than six and one half years, he has wielded power, and has displayed uncanny mastery of the objectors of his policies. He is a fighter. Don't count him out yet.

From left, Ukrainian President Leonid M. Kravchuk, Belarussian President Stanislav Shushkevich and Russian President Boris N. Yeltsin as they announced the creation of a commonwealth.

Reuters

2-9-91

Nuclear Threat Still Exists in Russia

In Washington, President Bush was told that the Ukraine, Russia and Belarus had formed a new commonwealth. The Secretary of State, Jim Baker, indicated the Soviet Union, as we have known it, no longer exists. Bush feels a loyalty to Mikhail Gorbachev, President of the Soviet Union, and he clearly favors dealing with a central government. The United States may be able to play a key role in determining what happens to Gorbachev.

Director of Russian studies at Georgetown University, Harvey Balzar, noted that the American Administration can sustain the President of the Soviet Union, by continuing to funnel aid through him. The commonwealth will probably want the reformer of the USSR to be their director, within certain limits.

U.S. officials desire assurances that the independent Republics would maintain some central control of military command, particularly over nuclear weapons. About 80 percent of the Soviet strategic weaponry are in the Russian

Federation, with the rest deployed in the Republics of Belarus, Ukraine, and Kazakhstan. Tactical arms are distributed more evenly across the Soviet Union.

In the event of a Civil War, a rebel group might threaten the outside world by capturing control of a strategic nuclear missile aimed at the West.

To prevent a nuclear tragedy, the Bush Administration recently provided 400 million dollars for the dismantling of nuclear weapons in Ukraine and Kazakhstan, delay the Soviet debt payment of 100 million dollars for food and supply grain credits, in addition to distribution of the aid package.

Representative of the House of Representatives, Lee Hamilton, for the United States, a Democrat from Indiana, is not persuaded that Yeltsin and the other Slavic leaders, are up to the task of forming a Commonwealth, under current conditions. Hamilton said, "They are untried." My impression is they have proven their political skills. Do they have ability to govern?

1-26-91
Russia Fights to Stabilize Economy
Austere budget may eliminate the chronic deficit by slashing defense spending. Allocations for arms purchases alone will be cut by 80 percent.

Deputy Prime Minister Yegor Gaidar, explained to lawmakers that only through a balanced budget, with sharp reductions in government subsidies, can Russia move from a state control to a free market economy. According to reliable sources, Gaidar acknowledged that the tough measures would bring pain and unemployment to a nation where prices of food and consumer goods have tripled in cost.

Alexander Pochinok, Chairman of the Legislature Budget Committee, demands a 65 percent increase in spending proposed by the government, to make up for the growth in prices; above all in agriculture, health care, general and higher education, mass media, and other spheres.

Soviets, critical of economic reforms, said that with great irony, "the vote by Parliament showed confidence in the Coalition, and the President," Boris Yeltsin. Russia's dependence on foreign aid gives it little choice but to adopt stringent austerity measures. Guidar intimated many donors require action in reforms. Grain imports, bought with western credits, and the group of seven industrial countries, agree to defer payments of the former Soviet Union's debts until the end of March. This will bring progress toward economic stabilization and a free market system.

President of Russia, Boris Yeltsin, has lifted restrictions on retail and wholesale trade. His new decree gives individuals and organizations the right to buy and sell goods, including street corners, without government permits. Trade by state cooperatives has been the biggest obstacle to privatization. Corrupt officials and underground business people have thrived like leeches on the state monopoly system for decades.

President Bush, third from bottom, addresses the Security Council at the United Nations on Friday as Russian President Boris Yeltsin, at far end of table, listens.

1-30-92
Yeltsin Proposes Reduction in Arsenal

Official sources say Boris Yeltsin of Russia proposes a sweeping disarmament reduction for strategic warheads, with cuts more than 80 percent.

The President of Russia will present his ideas to President George Bush of the United States at Camp David, Maryland, and will call for creation of a jointly operated global defense system. It would by similar to that envisioned in the American Strategic Defense Initiative, or "Star Wars" program, providing protection against nuclear attacks.

Conditions are now ripe for major steps in arms reduction, and Yeltsin has asked Great Britain, China, and France to unite behind the super powers to radically reduce their arsenals.

The Russian President at the United Nations Security Council in New York will give these specific actions. They will include ways to tighten controls on uranium, chemical and biological agents used in making weapons, and on technology with military and civilian purposes, and oversee weapons disarmament.

Russia is halting production of the long-distance Blackjack and Bear Heavy Bombers, stopping the manufacture of air and sea launched cruise missiles, and eliminating more than half of their nuclear armament Russia now holds. In addition, the Commonwealth nation will restrict ground maneuvers and boldly parallel or reciprocate action for further destruction of weapons deployed now, if the United States does.

Yeltsin intimated, "We are seeking to achieve the reasonable sufficiency of nuclear and conventional arms. The savings will be channeled to meet civilian needs and implement economic reform." Secretary of State, Jim Baker, said, "Both Presidents have offered proposals of significant consideration."

2-2-92
Partnership and Friendship Declared by Bush and Yeltsin

President Bush of the United States and Boris Yeltsin, President of Russia, met at Camp David, Maryland, and declared a formal end to seven decades of rivalry.

Officials present at the American Retreat said the two leaders reviewed the prospects for further support for Yeltsin's program of Democratic Reforms, and for arms control reductions to as low as 2500 nuclear warheads that each nation deploys.

No specific agreements were reached on either issue, but concrete proposals will be followed up in a Summit in the spring. Endorsing and signing a statement of cooperation lends prestige to Yeltsin as a leader of Russia. A retinue of senior aides, including a roster of advisers to Yeltsin, largely is unknown to the Americans. They are Russian Foreign Minister Andrei Kozyrev: Marshall Yevgeny Shaposhnikov, who commands the combined military of the Commonwealth of Independent States; and Yuli

Vorontosov, Chief Russian Delegate to the United Nations; Yevgeny Velikhov, Deputy Chairman of Russian Academy of Sciences; and Vladimir Lukin, the Ambassador-Designate of policy planning. He is also a senior advisor to Jim Baker, the American Secretary of State.

An issue of substance emerged from the session. An offer by Bush to set up a joint center in which scientists from the United States would pursue research with some 2000 or more Russian military experts who are being displaced by Yeltsin's sharp military cut backs.

Yeltsin said he enthusiastically supports the proposal, which is aimed at preventing the scientists from selling services to terrorists, or other nations seeking to develop a nuclear arsenal. Russia has begun offering raises and other benefits to keep them from leaving.

1-18-92
Yeltsin Convinces Military to Remain United

If other Republics force the military to break up and form their own armies, giant Russia is in the best position to create its own powerful armed force, and will do so, said Boris Yeltsin.
He announced that Russia is taking under its jurisdiction all troops located outside the Commonwealth: Lithuania, Latvia, Estonia, Georgia, as well as other parts not seeing independence. More than 5000 officers from the former Soviet army were present in Moscow, in the Kremlin, to hear Yeltsin claim, "we will fight to the death for unified military forces." The President of Russia explained to his audience his offer of 120,000 apartments on quarter acre plots. He smiled to them, and said, "Why aren't you reacting? Don't you like it?" Anticipating their concern about money to build on these plots, Yeltsin rubbed his hands together and promised them cash from the sale of surplus military equipment. The officers started to smile back, and applaud. Throughout the day, one officer after another trooped to the podium to voice their support to keep the 3.4 million member former Soviet military together.

One high-ranking officer said, "We do not want political aims, personal interests, and ambition of some short-sighted leaders to split us. Official sources indicated that air force Marshall Yevgeny Shaposhnikov, the interim Commander in Chief of the Commonwealth's armed forces, cautioned that in political terms, there must be a transition period of at least two to three years when there should be some joint command. He criticized the governments of the Ukraine, and other republics for moving too fast to create their own armies. So far, 68,000 former Soviets have taken a loyalty oath to the Ukraine, including 15,000 officers.

Yeltsin considers the joint command of strategic forces, agreed by the Commonwealth leaders to include the navy and the combined nuclear command.

Officers of the former Soviet military take a break from Kremlin meeting where they sought a unified command for the armed forces.

1-14-92
Who Controls the Black Sea Fleet?

Although Russia and the Ukraine have backed away from their dispute over who will inherit the powerful Black Sea Fleet, that once belonged to the Soviet Union, there is a threat: The military stability of the Commonwealth. Russia under Catherine the Great founded the naval force, now 350 vessels, and 70,000 sailors. The Crimea Peninsula, where its main base is located, was given to Ukraine in the 1950's. Both of the major Soviet Republics have adamantly laid claim to its force.

A panel of military experts is expected to resolve the standoff. Admiral Igor Kasatonov, the Fleet Commander, has asserted that the entire force, 45 battle vessels, 28 submarines, 300 medium sized ships and coastal craft, 151 airplanes, 85 helicopters, is strategic. It projects the Soviet influence in the Middle East and Asia. Tactical weapons are nuclear activated, and carried on some ships. They will be removed, and destroyed. The Admiral insists that the fleet should belong to the joint command, which includes Russia and the Ukraine.

Each of the Republics, eleven in all, has the right to form its own army. In another dispute, the Ukraine has demanded that all Soviet soldiers on its territory take a new oath of loyalty, which has angered other republics.

Whatever the ultimate share proves to be, much of it may be sold or scrapped. Ukraine officials, it is reported, have no intention of sending its ships into the Mediterranean.

General Kostantin Morozov, the Ukranian Defense Minister, argues that once tactical weapons are removed, the Black Sea fleet should no longer be considered a "strategic force," and its ownership should be renegotiated.

1-12-92
Commonwealth Responsibility

The admission of the Republic's Confederation in what was once the Soviet Union, has a responsibility to itself, and to the world if it is to succeed.

According to Jim Baker, Secretary of State of the American Nation, there are four criteria for unity; establish Democratic values and practices, protect human rights and minorities; respect borders and peaceful change and fulfill international obligations.

The larger republics, Ukraine, Belarus, and Kazakhstan, may see the Commonwealth as a halfway house, on the road to complete independence. Others may view it as a modest improvement over the Communist system.

The agreement does not explain how borders are to be demarcated, or who is responsible for their security. What does Commonwealth citizenship mean? These questions are unanswered. The United States faces two challenges: On the international scene, it should work closely with the Russian Republic, to prevent expansionism. On the other hand, we should not encourage Russian domination of the Republics in the Union.

A cadre of the Communist Party, adaptable to nationalistic slogans and Democratic rhetoric, is a tribute to their survival skills.

Do we really know enough about the players to take a stand? In the Soviet context, the issue of minorities merges with territorial claims. The American strategists should take care not to legitimize forcible seizure of disputed boundaries between the land east of the Dnieper and the Crimea in the Ukraine, to the Eastern part of the Belarus, to important regions of Latvia and Estonia. Commonwealth Republics should be treated like the European Community. They can enforce the spirit of cooperation, which will open up worldwide exchange.

1-2-92
Vance Mediates Cease Fire in Yugoslavia

An analyst reports that the envoy of United States, Cyrus Vance, who was the former Secretary of State, has made a declaration: both sides of this undeclared war between Serbia and Croatia, have accepted in full, in its entirety, a proposal for a cease fire.

In separate meetings Vance has spoken to the leader of Croatia, Tudjman, and Serbian President Milossevic, and they pledge their support for stationing as many as 10,000 foreign troops inside Croatia. The combatants will silence their guns in three areas. This will be the fifteenth truce since June 25, 1991, when the people of Croatia declared the Declaration of Independence. Hopefully the 400,000 refugees, who fled the war-torn area, will be able to return to their homes. At the present time, the Serbian Rebels control the region.

Serbia is widely viewed as the Chief Aggressor, and has been hit hard by a western trade embargo, that could end if peace is restored. Milosevic's power base is built on the promises of unity and security of all the Serbs. Renunciation of these policies would anger the guerilla factions and probably cause them to break the cease-fire.

The Croat Leader, Tudjman's future is even more uncertain. He is under intense pressure from radicals opposed to deployment of foreign troops. Many fear the United Nations, "Blue Helmets," will establish a new border that protects the Serbian conquests.

Insert Sunday, December 29, 1991 newspaper clipping here

Los Angeles Times

SUNDAY, DECEMBER 29, 1991
COPYRIGHT 1991 / THE TIMES MIRROR COMPANY / ★ / 328 PAGES

Associated Press

Mikhail Gorbachev greets well-wishers Friday while on a last Kremlin stroll. He quit as head of the defunct USSR on Wednesday.

12-18-91

Yeltsin Moves with Expediency to Takeover the Kremlin Radio and Television

Russian President, Boris Yeltsin, takes over the state radio and television broadcasting, and slashes the power of his Vice President. He also commandeered Mikhail Gorbachev's Kremlin office. By Presidental decree, Yeltsin renames the Soviet broadcasting company, Gosteleradio, to Ostankino, after a Moscow studio, with national exposure. Yegor Yakovlev, a proponent of journalistic openness, will stay on as its Chief of Operations.

Yeltsin moved into the Kremlin to Gorbachev's suite of offices, at displeasure of the former Soviet aides. The retired Soviet President, with no visible sign of embarrassment, went down a floor to the office of Grigory Revenko, who had been Gorbachev's Chief of Staff, to carry on his work.

Gorbachev plans to visit his mother, Maria, in his native Stravropol, Region of Southern Russia. The retired President will return to Moscow to organize the business of an international think tank, that he created after the uprising in August.

Yeltsin has decisively dealt with a critic, Russian Federation Vice President, Alexander Rutskoi, by stripping him of this control over five state committees. The Afghan hero has been increasingly vocal in denouncing what he calls intrigue and incompetence of Yeltsin's entourage; and he openly criticized the Russian leader's plan for freeing up prices, which is expected to result in a drastic loss of buying power for most of the populace.

How far has this revolution of change come? Glasnost, openness, presented by Gorbachev, has widened the doors of opportunity. Under the Communist rule, the business of permission to travel was tentative. It took at least six months to render a decision of the KGB, government control, for a Visa to be granted, said Rose Kostyuk, wife of a Russian Communist.

Yelstin Moves

Images of her life near the Afghan border flash like a kaleidoscope, pristine meadows alive with poppies, herds of sheep on parched hillsides, and her husband, vasya, a villager from Minsk, mounting a horse at daybreak, and riding off to inspect the cotton fields. Through all the injustices, she tried to hold onto a dream of a better world. Today she remembers the hardships, yet a joyful reunion in the United States with friends, after 30 years of depression, eating lobsters and real spaghetti seem to give her hope and renewed confidence for peace.

In the former Soviet industry, there is not a single project that does not have western technical assistance. Ford Motor Company helped design the auto plants. The Arthur McKee firm of Cleveland, Ohio helped build the steel works at Magnitogorsk in the Ural Mountains. International harvester and Caterpillar assisted in producing heavy equipment.

Dupont, RCA, "A who's who of Capitalist Industry," played a role, with German specialists even more prevalent. American coal miners, tool and die makers, American electricians, keep key equipment humming efficiently. It is the adventurism of the West that drives people into foreign lands, and the challenge of producing a quality product.

12-18-91
Soviet Union Ends – A Crisis of Legitimacy Grips the Commonwealth

On New Year's Eve, the Hammer and Sicle flag, of the Revolutionary Red that has flown for 74 years over the Kremlin, the Medieval fortress on the Moscow River, will be lowered, marking a formal end to the Soviet Era.

In its place will fly the Russian tri-color of blue, white and red; as the Kremlin becomes the seat, once again, of the Russian government. "The time has come for transition," said Gorbachev. He feels he has a duty to lead the nation through this period. He urged the national Supreme Soviet, the country's legislature, to hold a final meeting to approve a constitutional transformation.

The dissolution of the Soviet Union should be the occasion for reflection. Throughout the entire region of what was once known as the Soviet Bloc, a massive transformation is underway. The mechanism of central economic planning has collapsed before any replacement design or organized transition can be created. Spontaneous adjustments to market operations are being imposed with essentially no preparation. At the same time, methods of authority and political control have been ineffective.

Civil society, its institutions, legal structure, and public attitudes are in the development stage, however they need controls and standards. Legitimacy refers to willingness of people to accept authority and without controls, no political system can function.

The crisis in emerging governments is they are unable to collect taxes at the rate they inherit. Neither can they enforce decrees or uphold longstanding laws.

All the new states of the Commonwealth will require international engagement in reconstruction, and with market access.

12-17-91
What Will the Russian Commonwealth Be?

The Commonwealth of Russia is being formed with the blocks of the puzzle-identified day to day. Along the way, new leadership will have to resolve matters such as, who will get the seat of the Security Council? Who will control the diplomatic corps? How will the international arms control treaties be protected?

Foreign Minister, Eduard Shevardnadze said, "It is not the kind of process that needs two kinds of sittings and consultations, and coming up with a statement or draft agreement. It is a complex issue."

The overriding question is, according to Gabriel Shoenfeld of International Studies, is the most basic power. Each of the Republics has to grapple with how much to delegate to the center.

In the British Commonwealth, the center has no power at all, but in contrast, the twelve-nation European Community, another form of Commonwealth, started out a generation ago with power to regulate each of its member's policies on customs and tariffs. Ever since, the community's central institutions have slowly gained more clout, and by the end of the decade, European Community members now plan to delegate to the center broad authority over their economies, foreign policy and defense.

Opposition to the center has been in the heart of the Baltic; Estonia, Lithuania, and Latvia, and they have made it clear that they have no interest in joining the Commonwealth.

Both Yeltsin, President of Russia, and Gorbachev, Soviet President, sought to reassure the American Secretary of State, Jim Baker, that there will be continued tight control over the estimated 30,000 Soviet nuclear weapons. Kravchuk, President of Ukraine, said over the weekend that the four Republics with nuclear arsenals, should have no veto power over their use.

Commonwealth
Yeltsin Indicated that all four Republics will join the non-proliferation treaty, and will dismantle their weapons system. A new command structure must take place with conventional arms deployment soon. Maintenance of a central military command, with executive powers, is the best option.

Establishing a common currency will be a priority. Control over printing money is a key factor, and central banks, making available credit and controlling inflation.

12-12-91
Yeltsin Alliance Adds Two More Republics

Armenia and Kyrgyzstan have decided to join the "Commonwealth of Independent States," which will increase the chance that the alliance formed over the weekend by Slavic leaders will attract most of the Republics.

Top officials in five other Republics support the idea of a loose economic and strategic community, however they have not made a hard and fast commitment. The leaders of the five Republics, Uzbekistan, Kyrgyzstan, Ashkhabad, Kazakhstan, and Tadzhikstan are predominantly Muslim, and are expected to meet to discuss the issue today. Yeltsin, the President of Russia, reported he would travel to Alma-Ata, Capital of Kazakhstan, to sign agreements if they decide to be part of the Commonwealth.

In short, while the Soviet Union is ceasing to exist, it has not been replaced in all its functions. Gorbachev is not likely to revive the old Federal Union, or to gain acceptance to a confederation of Russian States, yet he is the residual leader still playing an important traditional role.

Gorbachev's position is critical. If he continues to bid support of the Soviet military, it could lead to fragmentation of the Armed Forces and possibly Civil War.

In a late memorandum of understanding, in a conversation with the President of the Ukraine, Kravchuk, he acquiesces with the President of the Soviet Union, Gorbachev, that the military forces will remain under a unified "control" of Moscow.

These developments dampen the threat of political divisiveness, between the old Soviet Union's Western Slavic Majority and Eastern Islamic Minority. It also groups the four Soviet Nuclear Republics together once more, under weapons control-treaties. Kazakhstan will be joining Russia, the Ukraine, and Belarus, or Byelorus Russia.

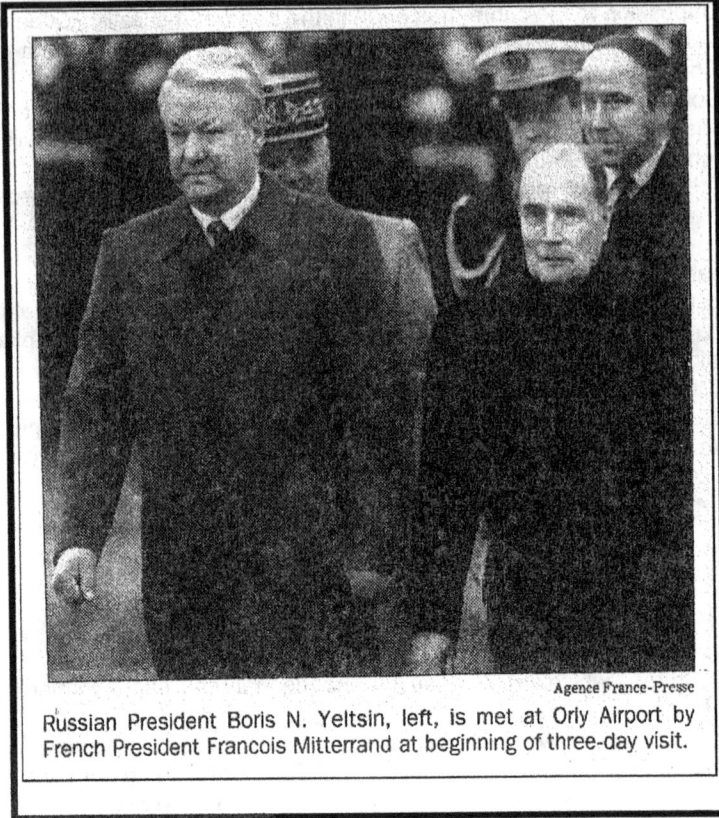

Russian President Boris N. Yeltsin, left, is met at Orly Airport by French President Francois Mitterrand at beginning of three-day visit.

2-6-92
Yeltsin Impressed with France's Mitterrand

France displays esteem for the Russian Head of State, Boris Yeltsin. The President of the largest, most powerful country in Asia, until the collapse of the Soviet Union, became the first leader invited to Paris since Czar Nicholas 2, in 1896, to cement a key element of European stability; "The Franco-Russian Entente."

The French President, Francois Mitterrand traveled to Orly airport, south of Paris, to greet his guest. A broad red carpet was spread on the pebble-strewed courtyard of Mitterrand's official residence, the Elesee Palace to welcome Yeltsin. Winding up his trip from Great Britain, America, and Canada, the Russian President thanked the French for support during his transition period. He is hopeful France will cut its nuclear supply arsenal. He will sign a pioneering treaty laying legal groundwork for future relations between the two countries.

Mitterrand escorted Yeltsin and his wife in a limousine through the streets of Paris by the mounted unit of the elite "Garde Republicaine" preceded by 20 horsemen blowing trumpets. The media reported that the boulevards of the capital were festooned with the flags of France, and the former Czarists red, white and blue, tri-color flag that serves Russia now. The couple was honored at the Grand Trianon Ballroom of the Versailles Palace.

Chaos, provoked by the disbanding of the former Soviet Union, has left more than 740 million dollars credit, allocated by France, frozen. In view of Russia's pressing economic problems, by abolition of government price support for consumer goods, Yeltsin is laying claim to the Lion's share of the credits. He is also counting on French cooperation in the field of management training.

LOS ANGELES TIMES

Associated Press

Russian President Boris N. Yeltsin, left, and French President Francois Mitterrand exchange treaties.

YELTSIN: French Economic Aid

2-7-92
Vacuum Created in Former USSR
Official source reveal that in terms of symbolic antagonists to American Democracy, the fall of Communism has left a cultural vacuum, and there is fear that nationalism may fill the emptiness.

When the Berlin wall crumbled, it released more than prisoners of the Marxist Regime; it also heralded a return to divisive nationalism that once riddled Europe. The dismemberment of Yugoslavia, and continuing border disputes escalated into separate racism, erupting and opening old   wounds of past centuries.

Through Gorbachev, the Americans have been able to dramatize and identify with events in the Soviet realm. The former leader of the Soviet Union was associated with a series of world-historical transitions, from the Cold War to a foreign partner; from colonizer to liberator; and from enemy to friend. Through him, an alien and threatened empire became an associate, able to work toward resolving their difficulties. The beginning of massive reforms brought about glasnost or openness.

Yeltsin's dramatic nuclear disarmament exceeds that of Gorbachev's most ambitious goals. The Russian President is attempting to close down the abusive Communist cooperatives, and begin a free market system. Inflation has caused the price of staples of bread and meat to rapidly increase. To prevent collapse, he has ordered his government to lower prices on staple goods. In addition, Yeltsin has eliminated their value-added tax, which make the food more affordable.

By decree, officials will increase pensions to their people by about 200 rubles per pensioner. A ruble is worth nearly two cents in American money. At this moment, almost 90 percent of the pensioners are below the poverty level, Minister of Social Affairs, Ella Panfilova, told the Legislature.

2-10-92

Red Guard Rises Out of the Ashes

Speakers in Moscow contrary to the reforms of Boris Yeltsin, demanded that the congress of the people's deputies be convened next month to restore Soviet leaders of last August's coup. Cries of long live Communism, the ideology of the populace, and placards openly blaming Russian-Jews and international Zionism for the countries economic woes were also raised during a rally in Moscow Red Square.

Eduard Salnikov, a construction worker commented, "What is happening now is not connected with the objective of a free enterprise system, or attempts to break through the market economy. It is plain and open extermination of the people. The pro-Communist rally is organized by a loose coalition of groups that include the Communist workers party and the Moscow labor unions.

Alexei Sergeyev, a leader of the Communist workers party, and a prominent Marxist Economist, suggested an alternative program for the Russian President. He calls for limits on profits of 15 percent, state control of foreign trade, seizure of hard currency holdings of private entrepreneurs: to buy food, and closure of small businesses profiting through resale of goods. Let the black market swindlers and speculators suffer, he added.

Official sources reveal that Colonel Viktor Alksnis, another leading hard-liner is less optimistic. He indicated the military would have to back the party of the Soviets to cause the downfall of the Commonwealth, and he doesn't see this action now.

To champion quick stimulus of their economy, Secretary of State, Jim Baker of the United States, arranged airlifts to bring food and medicine to the deprived people of the Commonwealth. Countries of the European states, Japan and the Far East nations participated. Baker said, "What happens there can affect other areas of our globe."

2-12-92
Russia Calls for End of Nuclear Arms
The five acknowledged nuclear powers should be put on zero alert, according to the leader of the Commonwealth states, and immediately take them off combat status. President Boris Yeltsin said that Russia and the United States should take the first step, but ultimately the international organization should control the remaining nuclear weapons.

In addition, the Russian President suggested the United Nations create a special police force to protect the human rights around the world. Andrei Kozyrev, Russian Foreign Minister, indicated possible steps could include economic and other sanctions. One can consider the question of establishing police security specially trained for such operations. Total elimination of destructive armament cannot be done overnight, but through step by step cutbacks, according to Kozyrev.
Yeltsin's plan is bolder. Separation of nuclear warheads from missiles, planes, ships and submarines, can guarantee their unauthorized or accidental use. Extensive verification measures should be provided to prevent cheating.
The Russian President also renewed his call for a global space-based missile defense system, operated by the nuclear power countries, however there is always a threat from adventurers, irresponsible politicians, and terrorists. Officials report that Yeltsin is seriously considering having a separate army, and he will issue a decree after he has informed the leaders of the 11 former Soviet Republics that make up the Commonwealth of Independent States. Dmitry Volkogonov, General and Russian Military Advisor, indicated Russia would not need more than 1.5 million men. Commonwealth members have been unable to decide on structure, and legal basis for funding a joint strategic force. As to tactical weapons, they are in agreement that all the nuclear missiles will be located on Russian territory, complete by mid-summer.

Los Angeles Times

SUNDAY, FEBRUARY 16, 1992
COPYRIGHT 1992 / THE TIMES MIRROR COMPANY / ● / 478 PAGES

Russian President Boris Yeltsin speaks with leaders of the Commonwealth of Independent States in Minsk, Belarus, Fri- day. The Commonwealth leaders were meeting to discuss the structure, composition and financing of CIS armed forces.

Associated Press

55

2-15-92
Eight Republics Remain United

Belarus and Uzbekistan will join a post-Soviet military alliance; a two-year transition period but will reaffirm their intent to create their own armies, for different reasons. The meeting of the Commonwealth of Independent States signaled the dissolution of the 3.7 million-member Soviet Armed Forces; the world's largest for decades that imitated other nations.

The Commonwealth will be defined as an economic rather than a military union. Russian President, Boris Yeltsin, considered it better to keep intact as much of the former military as possible, to enhance his own countries security, and to assuage an angry officer corps that is starting to show signs of dissatisfaction.

The strategic force will have the old Soviet Nuclear Arsenal, most of the air force, its air defense and early warning and intelligence-gathering systems; all under the command of Shaposhnikov, the Commander-in-Chief. There will be a deputy for conventional forces, and a third person as Chief of Staff. The deputies will be confirmed at the Summit in Kiev on March 20.

The two Republics that joined the Ukraine, and refused to participate in the joint alliance have their reasons for wanting their own army. Azerbaijan hopes to halt the ethnic clashes around Nagorno-Karabahk, an Armenian enclave, in Azerbaijan. Belarus sovereignty is primary to them, and they resive to be a nuclear-free neutral state.

Meantime in Chelyabinsk, Russia, Jim Baker, the American Secretary of State, has been invited to see their top-secret laboratory that once designed Soviet nuclear bombs. The United States and Germany are negotiating with the Russian Government to create a scientific clearinghouse to sponsor peacetime projects. Vladislav Nikitin, the facilities Deputy Director, pointed out that none of the scientists had left the Institute.

2-20-92
Ambassador to Russia Offers Ideas

Robert Strauss, Envoy of Russia, has an idea on how to reverse Soviet Socialism; open a dozen grocery stores.

People there need food. We can make food and medicine available to them through the free market system. Entrepreneurs will find suppliers willing to sell at prices the individuals will pay. Strauss said, "This is what I am here for, what I set out to do; make it happen. You may ask, why grocery stores? Because, this Texan's father ran a dry goods store in the United States, and he was aware of the incentive to produce a product for a fair market value, and became successful. They can do the same."

The monopolies of the former Communist regime are a major barrier to the new vision Strauss projects. It has been difficult to privatize the State government corporate position. They use every means they can think of to torpedo free enterprise.

Other projects Strauss is involved with is reviews with Deputy Prime Minister Yegor Gaidar, in investment banking. Moving American oil companies into Siberian oil fields to boost production, and shutting down marginal wells;

concentrating on those that can be improved is important for them to produce quick hard currency earnings.

Having American specialists give advice on handling, packaging, and storage of agricultural products will reduce loss that may sometimes be a quarter of their harvest.

The Ambassador stated, "Aid should come to them in loans, not outright assistance, and pledge natural resources to pay loan."

2-24-92
Communists Protest Glasnost – Openness

Protesters are chanting, "Yeltsin, resign;" and calling for a "return of Soviet power." The demonstrators were beaten with rubber truncheons as they tried to shove their way past police barricades, making their way to Moscow's main shopping avenue, Tverskaya Street.

About 3000 protestors carried Soviet red flags and portraits of Bolshevik leaders, Lenin and Stalin. They demanded to hold a rally in honor of Red Army Day, now called Armed Services Day, outside the walls of the Kremlin. Meanwhile, less than two blocks away, the Russian President, Boris Yeltsin, Vice President Alexander Rutskoi, and other military officers were placing wreaths at the tomb of the Unknown Soldier, next to the Kremlin wall.

The United Brown and Red Forces, in other words anti-Yeltsin alliance of various chauvinistic groups, wanted to provoke an incident and blame the government. They nearly succeeded. Over the last two months, there was been a growing attempt to overthrow the fragile commonwealth of independent states. The ultra-conservatives are desperate and disenchanted with the free enterprise movement.

One veteran, Vladimir Adisonov, wiped tears of humiliation and anger from his eyes, after being flailed unceremoniously by a policeman said, "I spent 40 years in the Armed Forces, most of my life, and I am here to honor my friends of the past, V.I. Lenin, and Joseph Stalin." How can America support Yeltsin? We are not yet organized, but we will be.

2-25-92
How Democratic is Russia?

According to Mikhail Gorbachev, Stalinist Communist in the Soviet Union ignored human rights, dignity and human needs. This was a system that did violence to society and perverted the ideas of Socialism.

Socialism can live on. The desire to experiment and to find a new form for putting Socialist ideas into practice is on going. Embracing Democratic and humanitarian principles is a quest our country should strive for, added Gorbachev.

Jean Kirpatrick, former Ambassador, indicates it is not enough for the United States and the West to reduce armed forces; cut the defense budgets, or assist in dismantling the nuclear arsenals of the Soviet Union of the past. It is critically important that they make room for Russia and the other democracies. The European Community has resisted a closer economic and political association sought by Poland, Hungary, and Czechoslovakia. The United States has resisted expanding NATO's North Atlantic peace organization membership, and to extend guarantees to include the Eastern Bloc. The Democrats have been slow to grant economic assistance and security arrangements, added Kirpatrick.

Given time and freedom, the countries of the Commonwealth of Independent States and Eastern Europe will find their way to a free and fair enterprise system and prosper, yet will the authoritarians allow this to happen? Impatience may cut short the democratic experiment. A restoration of a dictatorship in Russia may once again deprive the people of self-government.

By his acts, Boris Yeltsin, President of Russia, has demonstrated his will for peace and freedom. The world leaders must make a place for the new democracies.

GARY FRIEDMAN / Los Angeles Times
President Boris N. Yeltsin besieged by reporters. What he tells them depends heavily on what his advisers say.

3-21-92
A Battle Emerges for Boris Yeltsin

Maneuvering carries a crucial significance, as other parts of a typical checks-and-balance system of government have yet to mature.

The constitutional court, which has powers to invade Yeltsin's decrees, began work last month. Russia remains in constitutional limbo, and the fate of the new constituency is to be decided in the Russian Congress in April.

Political parties remain splintered, unruly, and virtually powerless with local elections postponed. Public opinion has few direct channels of influence on the government, and the exception only is extreme form strikes and riots.

Yeltsin has staked his political authority on economic reforms by becoming his own Prime Minister, and he was appointed Yegor Gaidar as his Deputy to run the reforms, and promised him a free hand, and unflinching support. When in December, Yeltsin finished off the Soviet Union by agreeing with the Ukraine and Belarus to form the Commonwealth States.

The political domination shifted decisively to what some analysts call the young Turks, 30-50 years old, who have thrown off their Communist past. With Burbulis, a former Marxism Professor, and Guidar Shakhrai, a lawyer who oversees the legal aspects of Yeltsin's decrees, he has a strong coalition. Along with these powerful leaders is the Minister of Justice, Labor and the Media, is Andrei Kozyrev.

The Prime Minister's advisor and Chief of the Central Government is Alexei Golovkov. He has to deal with powerful lobbies from the collective farm chairman, who tries to block land reform. Also there are military factories, fighting for defense funds, and businessmen agitating for lower taxes, or exemptions. Without the backing of full-fledged classes of businessmen and private farmers, he is doomed, says Vera Kuznetsova, Reporter of Nezavismaya.

4-6-92
Kravchuk of the Ukraine Moves to Take Over the Black Sea Fleet

Sources in the Ukraine said tensions are aggravated between Leonid Kravchuk and Yeltsin, as he issues a decree to seize the Black Sea Fleet, putting all military and naval forces in the Ukrainian territory under his government.

A potent force of 90,000 men, 345 surface ships, 28 submarines, and 159 warplanes; Russia claims them as its inheritance from the former Soviet Union. The issue brings full confrontation, one of national pride and importance; and wealth for the sheer value of the fleet. With an angry exchange comes the real risk that the Commonwealth of Independent States, which groups Russia, the Ukraine, and nine other former Soviet Republics; will be permanently damaged.

Kravchuk is insistent on creating his own armed forces, for the basic military reason of protecting his own integrity as a power to contend with. The republic has sworn in about a half million men, but feels the task is incomplete as long as a foreign army is on its land.

Yeltsin, the Russian President, has warned a unilateral action would bring Russian retaliation, and his country would not be intimidated. In supporting Kravchuk's decree, the leadership of the Ukrainian Parliament vowed the state was taking only a portion of what rightfully belonged to them.

The President of Russia issued a decree of his own that sharpens the conflict but left room for an eventual compromise. Yeltsin ordered the fleet in the Black Sea to hoist the cross of Saint Andrew, the traditional banner of the Russian Navy, in demonstration of their loyalty to Moscow. In a showdown, the Black Sea captains are believed to be loyal to Moscow, and would probably put to sea if Yeltsin ordered them to.

4-12-92
Kremlin Power Struggle in Moscow Loses Round

In Moscow, the Western-Minded members of Russia's government emerged as the victors and their conservative critics bowed to Yeltsin, as he overpowered them with his intent to dissolve the ministerial staff.

Foreign Minister of Trade, Pyotr Aven, one of the winners, said happily: after two days of haggling, the Russian people's deputies adopted a formal support for the pro-market being steered by the President of Russia.

A total of 578 Deputies in the Parliament voted in favor of the Declaration. With the Congress now accepting a share of political blame for painful social costs incurred by the race to a supply and demand economy, first Deputy Premier Yegor Gaaidar, chaired a forty-minute meeting of his ministers to order the next round of economic changes.

The government is preparing to phase out taxes on investments, probably starting this summer. Gaaidar extended an olive branch to the Parliament by stating we do not need a confrontation between the legislative and executive powers. Yeltsin can remain as head of the Government of Russia, and he retains his decree-making powers, however, the decision to nominate a new Prime Minister by mid July remains the same, and could serve as a rallying point for the President's political enemies.

This was an important decision for the Commonwealth of Independent States to remain united as aid from the International Monetary Fund, composed of the Commonwealth of Independent Nations may grant membership, a prerequisite of the funding in the amount of thirty billion dollars. Camdessus, Head of the International Monetary Fund, cautioned the size and effectiveness of any aid effort will depend on the speed with which the new nations put their economic reform programs into place.

4-22-92
Anti-Reform Communists Power Threat

The Russian people's congress of deputies have left the President of Russia, Boris Yeltsin's reforms alive, but under heavy siege. The members of the Congress, elected to a five-year term, reflect political realities of the immediate past. Former Communist functionaries are heavily represented in the 1046 member Parliament, where they form a powerful obstructionist bloc. Yeltsin, though he retains the power to rule by decree in key areas, was pressured to make concessions to the anti-reform faction. This may lead to a dilution in slowing the painful measures he advocates freeing the economy from the dead hand of centralized control.

Any slackening of momentum to a market economy, whether privatizing land and state enterprises, or eliminating price controls, and ending expensive subsidies might jeopardize the vital aid package that the United States, Western Europe and others are putting together.

Divided government often produces drift and inaction, even in the most established democracies. There is antagonism between the executive and legislative agencies that could be crippling, however Secretary of State, James Baker of America clearly stated that the interests and values are best served by seeing democracy and free markets take hold in Russia. This means supporting the forces of reform again
st the forces of reaction. Yeltsin remains the key instrument of their reform.

A4   WEDNESDAY, JUNE 24, 1992 ★

Russia and Ukraine Hail Friendship

■ **Commonwealth:**
Yeltsin, Kravchuk partly resolve dispute over Black Sea Fleet. They will join in talks Thursday on warfare in Moldova.

By VIKTOR GREBENSHIKOV
and CAREY GOLDBERG
SPECIAL TO THE TIMES

DAGOMYS, Russia—The leaders of Russia and Ukraine, smoothing relations that had threatened to explode the Commonwealth of Independent States, emerged from their first summit meeting Tuesday proclaiming new heights of friendship and cooperation.
    "Never before has there been so complete an understanding between Russia and Ukraine," Russian President Boris N. Yeltsin told vacationers who crowded around him in this Black Sea resort town.

Reuters
Ukrainian President Leonid Kravchuk, left, and Russian President Boris N. Yeltsin take a break for a beach stroll in Dagomys, Russia.

6-24-92
Renewed Comradeship with Russia and the Ukraine

In Dagomys Russia, the leaders of the Ukraine and Russia improved relations that had threatened to divide the Commonwealth of Independent States. An open understanding between Boris Yeltsin of Russia and the Ukraine President

Leonid Kravchuk, took place on the Black Sea resort town of Dagomys. The two leaders managed to resolve their persistent dispute over how to split the Black Sea fleet. Now, they jointly will operate the bases on the Crimean Shores and eventually create both a Ukrainian and a Russian Fleet.

The Summit meeting with President Bush of the United States boosted the prestige of Yeltsin. Control of nuclear weapons was a sticking point. Kravchuk did agree to seep rapid ratification of all nuclear treaties his country had committed, and would get rid of the strategic nuclear arms by the end of 1994. Russia would gradually introduce customs posts, and retain a no-Visa program.

In another peace initiative, Yeltsin is scheduled to meet with Georgian leader, Eduard Shevardnadze to discuss the bloodshed in the enclave of South Ossetia. Continuing his diplomatic barnstorming, the President of Russia is expected to sign a treaty on cooperation among countries bordering the Black Sea.

Yeltsin acknowledged that relations among the Commonwealth have been strained, but with the path of friendship, cooperation and cordiality with the Ukraine, a full scale political treaty may be signed.

7-6-92
Economic Summit at Munich Germany

President Bush of the United States will try to boost the stability of the American State with the group of seven at a Summit conference. He will attempt to get Germany to reduce their interest rates, hoping that the rest of the world powers will lower their rates also. Japan has already pledges to raise public spending to revive its domestic economy. The President of the United States hopes to avert a relapse of the United States employment status. Bush may be threatened with unemployment himself after the November election.

The G7 meeting will include the President of Japan, Germany, Italy, Prime Minister of Britain, Premier of France, Prime Minister of Canada, and the President of the United States. Now the Soviet Union has split into fifteen independent states, and it is important for them that there be agreement of social, economic, trade, and cultural activities.

We will watch interest rates. They are high at the Bundesbank in Germany. The West Germans are pumping 100 billion dollars into former East Germany. High interest rates hurt the American economy, and also add to the world recession. If the German Deutschmark weakens this summer, the dollar will gain in value, and this will spur economic growth in the U.S.

It is good to watch what Japan will do to clear its fraud of its high ranking officials, and if it will agree to give as much as 10 billion dollars to Russia. In return, the four Kuril Islands north of Hokkaido that the Soviet Union seized at the end of World War II will be given back to Japan.

The Summit will probably conclude with declarations of confidence and pledges of growth. How much the United States benefits this summer and fall is unpredictable, like the election itself.

7-18-92
American Challenge for the Presidency

In the United States, the Democratic Party has chosen their representative for the Presidency of the Country. Governor Bill Clinton of Arkansas is the unanimous choice. His Vice-President elect will be Al Gore of Kentucky, an environmental enthusiast. After thirty years of attempting to unify the party with a concrete agenda for changing the way government runs the nation, it has happened.

Governor of Virginia, Douglas Wilder, spoke of economy for a nation out of touch with reality. Rev. Jesse Jackson came aboard the train with the nomination of Al Gore for Vice-President, also voting for change. Jerry Brown previous Governor of California said the Republican Congress should be limited in the number of years the members run, a mention was two terms in office. Russ Perot, a candidate for a third independent party, announced he would not seek the office of President of the United States. There was plenty of attention for George Bush of the present administration, but not the kind he wanted. New York Governor, Mario Cuomo, said, "Step aside George Bush, you have had your parade."

Senator Bill Bradley of New Jersey, repeated to the delegation in New York City, Mr. President, you have waffled, wiggled, and wavered. With the Vice-President elect, Al Gore, he stated, "George, it is time for you to go."

The democrats presented to the audience and television video that Clinton came from an underprivileged background, and he went to Oxford in England on a Rhodes Scholarship. Cuomo related that Clinton was born poor, and survived the trauma of a difficult youth. The single most effective line in Clinton's acceptance speech was this simple statement, "I never met my Father." He had to struggle against overwhelming odds with an alcoholic stepfather. The theme for the campaign to the presidency is "change."

The American Presidency

The democratic nominee added that the American people want change, but the government is in the way. It had been hijacked by privileged, special interests; it is taking more of your money and giving you less service. The choice we offer now is not conservative or liberal, Democratic or Republican, it is working together to bring this nation together, without the rhetoric.

Barbara Jordan, a school teacher and past representative in Congress indicated we couldn't tax and spend our way to prosperity. An us-against-them tactic would not work. Unity is what would bring our country out of recession.

Governor Clinton referred to a new covenant, explained in the Bible by Isaiah; "Where there is no vision, the people will parish." Clinton's new government contains a public investment and expanded state services. Free college education, industrial training apprenticeship for any American who wants one; however the vital word in the Governor's program the "new covenant also collects." In return for a college education, it will require two years of public service, in the police, in schools, health or public welfare. The unemployed will get education and training, and childcare, but they will have to take whatever job they are given within two years. Individual responsibility is the key to a successful elimination of our national debt. With a reform of the health system, government jobs for the transport sector, such as roads, bridges, and infrastructure, the United States can recover and be a country we can be proud of. Money will be spent overwhelmingly on goods made in America, for America.

Los Angeles Times

SUNDAY, JULY 19, 1992
COPYRIGHT 1992/THE TIMES MIRROR COMPANY / ★ /444 PAGES

Associated Press

Democratic candidate Bill Clinton is showered with confetti as he leaves a New York hotel to start a 1,004-mile bus campaign.

12-13-92
Boris Yeltsin Survives Attack

Any political obituaries against the President of Russia are premature. He has called for a national referendum on his governance, and has put his opponents on notice he will not hesitate to take his case directly to the people. Despite enormous difficulties, strenuous opposition, and miscalculations, Yeltsin, his rebuffed Prime Minister, Yegor Gaaidar; and their associates, he has created new political realities that make return to the past unlikely.

Thousands of Communist party stalwarts, and functionaries of the military complex, have demanded that power be transferred to a national salvation committee. The leader, Alexander Tizyakov, organized a failed coup that landed Boris Yeltsin in leadership and change to a Democratic form of government in Russia.

Many powerful industry captains have managed to privatize their enterprises, and see their personal interests better served by a liberal economic system. Yeltsin has scored a more important victory by passing a constitutional amendment making it legal for the first time since 1917 for Russian citizens and corporations to buy, own and sell land and natural resources. The President of Russia has also taken decisive steps toward demilitarizing their economy by slicing military spending; reducing procurements this year by 70% from last years level.

In privatization, through vouchers, distributed to the population, in just over a month after its inception, 6000 large concerns, with 15 million workers have submitted applications. The transfer of small business to private entrepreneurs is progressing even faster. In Moscow, St. Petersburg, and Nizhni Novgorod, 350,000 apartments and numerous restaurants are privatized.

The Author - Clete Hinton

The author, Clete Hinton was born in a small town outside of Chicago, Illinois, March 12, 1925. His formative years were spent in Topeka, Kansas, where his father worked on the Santa Fe Railroad. He grew up in an atmosphere of competition and survival in a township called Highland Park. His family moved to California previous to the bombing of Pearl Harbor by the Japanese in 1941. His high school and junior college years were in Southern California in Long Beach and Compton, California. He also attended R.O.T.C. Military in Long Beach.

Mr. Hinton served in the Armed Forces in the Navy after graduation from high school from 1943 to 1946. The Author joined the Los Angeles County Fire Department in August of 1949, and worked for nearly 29 years, retiring as an engineer. He studied for his Associates of Arts degree, majoring in Fire Science, Hydraulics, and Business Administration.

After retirement in 1978, Mr. Hinton wrote a few articles for "Firehouse Magazine," edited by a New York firefighter, Dennis Smith.

The Author has studied Foreign History and done extensive research in the Middle East Theater involving Israel and her neighbors. Most of his writing is factual and in chronological order. This writing, Ard Of Crisis 1979" is a continuation of his previous book "The Return of the Sinai from 1979," Which is a sequal of his book, "The Camp David Accords."

www.ingramcontent.com/pod-product-compliance
Lightning Source LLC
Chambersburg PA
CBHW052107270326
41931CB00012B/2917